THE SIX PILLARS OF A REWARDING LIFE

A POWERFUL APPROACH TO TAKING ACTION
AND LIVING WITH DIRECTION

Copyright © 2022 by Blake de Vos

All rights reserved.

No part of this book may be reproduced in any form or by any electronic or mechanical means, including information storage and retrieval systems, without written permission from the author, except for the use of brief quotations in a book review.

Read.Think.Listen. Newsletter

Short Meaningful Words

Human Performance Tips

Inspirational Quotes From Others

WEEKLY WORDS TO IMPROVE THE QUALITY AND TRAJECTORY OF YOUR LIFE

Inside each edition:

- Two tips on improving your performance
- Short impactful words of wisdom
- Two quotes from others to inspire action

Thought provoking words you can read in under two minutes. Delivered direct to your inbox every Friday.

Join for free at: www.blakedevos.com/read-think-listen

To my parents, Christine and Henk. Thank you for your endless support each day and through altering stages of my life. This book would be nothing without you and your guidance over the years.

To Nicole, the love of my life. Thank you for showing me what it means to be resilient, compassionate and full of life.

To my friends and family. Thank you for showing interest throughout the process of writing this book, and thank you for always listening when I needed an ear. I'm grateful to know I have people by my side through the good and the tough times. You're greatly appreciated.

And finally, to you — the reader. Thank you for taking the time to read this book. May you live a full life, as defined by you.

CONTENTS

What Got Me Here — ix

PILLAR I
UNDERSTAND YOURSELF

1. Check Your Ego — 9
2. Appreciate Your Emotions — 14
3. Change And New Experiences — 20
4. All We Consume — 24
5. The Antidote To Fear — 30
6. Start To Live — 34
7. Understand Yourself: Summary — 41

PILLAR II
THE CHOICES YOU MAKE

8. Decision Mechanics And The Process Of Deciding — 49
9. Having Too Many Choices — 63
10. Be The Architect — 71
11. When Overthinking Occurs — 78
12. Learn To Play The Long Game — 85
13. Decide To Make An Impact — 90
14. The Choices You Make: Summary — 97

PILLAR III
ACHIEVING WHAT YOU SEEK

15. Creating A Pathway — 103
16. Your Motivations — 113
17. Setting Effective Goals — 118
18. Powerful Stages Of A Personal Challenge — 125
19. The Pitfalls Of Goal Setting — 134
20. Achieving What You Seek: Summary — 138

PILLAR IV
DEVELOPING EFFECTIVE HABITS

21. Habits and The Basic Science — 143
22. Shaping Your Identity — 152
23. The Relationship With Your Environment — 158
24. Starting Small — 164

25. Your Rewards And Motivators   171
26. Developing Effective Habits: Summary   175

PILLAR V
OPTIMAL PERFORMANCE

27. Initial Belief   181
28. How To Practise   187
29. The 1%   194
30. Energy And Performance   197
31. Productive Living   205
32. Our Ability To Procrastinate   211
33. Organised Success   219
34. Optimal Performance: Summary   222

PILLAR VI
LIVING IN THIS WORLD

35. Practise Patience   227
36. Pursue A Career Instead Of A Job   231
37. Become Someone Who Creates   234
38. Find Your Balance   237
39. Universal Lessons To Live A Good Life   241
40. Live A Rewarding Life   244

Read.Think.Listen   245
Acknowledgments   247
Please Leave A Review   249
Resources   251
About The Author   257

WHAT GOT ME HERE

We all have certain memories that stay with us. Some are good, and others we prefer to forget. Those memories give us a sense of continuity as we move through time. They provide details of who we are and who we'd like to be. When you're in deep thought, you can find those memories you circle back to. It could be the memory of starting your first job, or perhaps the time you felt replaceable in a job you loved. One thing I've realised is that we can use the positive and negative memories we engage with as a platform to improve the trajectory of our lives.

The memory that had consistently come back to me as I transitioned into adulthood came from when I was in Year 10. One afternoon, my English teacher sent me outside for disrupting the class. I waited outside, but it wasn't long before he came out screaming, "When is this going to stop?! The way you're going, you won't even pass basic English! You have no chance of graduating high school!"

It hit me. My eyes started to well up with tears as I succumbed to the intense pressure school had around my ability to perform. Multiply this pressure with the issues I had at home, and you have what most Year 10 students have at that age: doubt and lack of direction. There were no university aspirations, no thoughts about what I would do if I graduated Year 12. I just enjoyed playing sport and socialising. It wasn't as if my school didn't provide learning resources—they did. My motivation for progression ultimately came down to where I directed my attention.

I wasn't a privileged child growing up, but I felt privileged as a teenager. My mum was a single mother supporting my sister and I in my first few years until she met someone who changed the trajectory of my life. He became my dad during my childhood—someone I didn't have when I was born—and he took on the responsibility of providing a better life for his children. My parents worked hard enough for me to go to a prestigious school with plenty of career opportunities. But looking back, I never took advantage of those opportunities. I'm controversially content with that outcome because my many different experiences led me to becoming a writer.

During my schooling years, when most people were taking extra tertiary classes for university acceptance, I was just trying to make it to graduation. My maths class involved writing an essay to solve problems. And in my English class, amongst the bickering and boisterous nature of the group, I was never fully engaged in learning. I honestly don't even remember several of my teachers' names.

My attention span was, and still is, continuously trying to scramble its way back to the present. I scraped through Year 12, graduating in 2007. I don't know how. I don't think the school wanted to leave anyone behind. After graduating, I worked as a receptionist at a gym where I had been doing work experience throughout my final years of school. I ended up studying Fitness Certificate 3 and 4 in addition to the role as a health consultant at the same gym. It was my first introduction into "the real world". I still hold some of my favourite memories and friends from that job ten years later. I barely passed my fitness studies as my lecturers noted I had underachieved and underperformed. In hindsight, there was a consistent theme in my teenage years: I struggled to learn, and I struggled to apply.

After graduation, I continued my role as a health consultant and was the youngest worker at the gym.

By twenty, I became increasingly confident in my role and developed a liking for business, which stemmed from monthly budgets and an introduction to key performance indicators (KPIs). As confidence in my job grew, so did my motivation to learn. I applied as a mature age student to university with the intention to study business. I had no tertiary admission qualification from high school, which meant I had to apply for a STAT test—a scaled test to distinguish whether I was competent enough to study at a university level. With this test, there's no pass or fail score. You pay around two hundred and sixty dollars to sit the test and the score scale represents the differing degrees of abilities in the test itself.

A few weeks later, the results came through and I was offered admission into my second preferred school, Curtin University, studying commerce and majoring in finance and management. Admission infused me with motivation. However, those feelings quickly began disintegrating.

Towards the end of my first semester the struggle arrived at full force. I failed Economics 100 and barely scraped through Law 100 and Marketing 100. My confidence dropped as I weighed up whether or not university was for me. After some reflection, I stayed the course but failed three classes in the first year of my degree. My confidence was so low I had no interest in being on campus and consistently found it difficult to retain information. Every time I sat down in the library, doubt would creep in over my ability to apply what I was attempting to learn. My mind would cast forward, where I would envision sitting in an exam room, unsure of how to answer the questions.

Something needed to change. I didn't want to give up, considering the amount of university debt I already acquired, followed by the perceived disappointment my family would feel if I quit. The change I needed came from my interest in a student exchange program. At the time, I felt the only way to stay the course was to take my studies elsewhere. Looking back, I saw it as an opportunity to not only travel, but to start fresh without the pressure of failing in my hometown.

I always wanted to visit the USA, an enormous country with plenty of sport, an attractive culture and accessible travel opportunities. I applied for a student exchange program and was offered the opportunity to study overseas. In 2012 I flew to Louisville, Kentucky, a Midwest state in North America which, at the time, had a population of less than one million people. I arrived in Louisville, setting myself up for what was to come. It was one of the most rewarding experiences of my life.

I received higher grades in both my finance and management subjects than I had back in my hometown Perth. When I reflect back, I ask myself what the difference was. First, it was *how* I was taught. The way I was learning wasn't based on right or wrong. Teamwork and applying knowledge to real life situations overruled equations and theories. Second, and more importantly, I creatively pursued knowledge. The experience of a new environment and the feeling of having a sense of freedom allowed me to open my mind up and prove that the first year of university didn't define how I showed up and performed each day. Even though I returned to Perth and failed more classes, I didn't allow myself to cave under the perceived and forced pressure I felt in Year 10 and my first year of university.

I eventually dropped my studies back to part time, left my job at the gym and engaged in full-time work as a storeman for a company that distributes personal protective equipment (PPE) and workwear to the mining and construction sector. I applied for this role hoping to be promoted until I graduated from university. It took me six months working in the warehouse before being offered the role of junior account manager. After taking the opportunity, I made a promise to myself: I would still graduate. It took me seven years to complete a three-year degree —failure after failure, distraction after distraction, but ultimately action after action.

Today, how I think about living a rewarding life is much different than what it used to be. My path from directionless student to fulfilled author required many areas of focus. As my direction became clearer, I reduced the amount of pressure I placed on myself to perform in all aspects of my life by focusing on small improving behaviours and appreciating life for what it is: experience, learning, fun and purpose. And these aspects of life are exactly what I aim to convey in this book.

From when I first put the idea about being an author in my head until now, I've realised two things:
1. You can make time and focus on what matters every day.
2. When you take action on something you enjoy, you open up a world of opportunity and freedom.

We're always reacting to what we learn and continuously filtering out what is necessary and irrelevant.
One of the unfortunate truths I've come to understand is that society continually puts us in a box of outdated advice and unnecessary expectations. I believe with each new generation of living, there comes a new generation of learning. We've been conditioned through our learning years to perform to others' expectations instead of forging our own path. If you asked your friends what they remember from their days at university or high school, it would be the friendships they made and the experience of being in an environment where they could be themselves. Most students wouldn't remember their assignments or scores they received on their exams.
What's even more unfortunate is moving into a career where 'professionalism' trumps who we are as a person. This isn't to say that professionalism shouldn't exist. But for many of us, we're confined to expectations which contradict who we really are. It's not until we leave a professional environment and come home to our partner, roommate or family that we switch back to being ourselves.

Current society puts forward a three-stage life: learn, work, retire. We're shown a learning system based on right or wrong, yes or no—contributing towards our inability to act on our invested interests or pursue new ideas. This learning system is what ultimately leads us to continue on the path of an unwanted lifestyle, losing our ability to wake up each morning with intent and purpose. This book goes beyond the classrooms, beyond the passive learning we're required to memorise and regurgitate onto exam papers.

I instil six pillars which provide the confidence to find out what's important to you and how you can leverage your lifestyle to forge your own path. And if you already know what's important to you, this book aims to help refine your life so you reap the rewards from what you put in. But for many of us, we seek direction. We need understanding and clarity.

Do you want to write a book but don't know where to begin? This book is for you.

Are you contemplating changing careers but feel stuck on where to go? This book is for you.

Do you want to learn a new skill but you're low in confidence? Then this book is also for you.

Each pillar represents a powerful stepping stone to a world where you create opportunities and take complete, conscious control in your approach to living a rewarding life.

We often believe we cannot achieve or progress because we aren't good enough or don't know how to begin. This book articulates realisations that question what it is you seek in this world. Throughout these chapters, you'll find real-life stories, research, experiences and examples of effective solutions that are easy to implement.

I don't consider myself to have all the answers—I never will.

What I hope to provide for you is a book which brings confidence and direction so you can take action and give yourself the rewarding life you deserve. This book offers practical advice and self-reflective questions that encourage you to break through your limiting beliefs and leverage your actions so you can wake up each day with a plan towards freedom.

One of the most remarkable superpowers within our ability to learn new things is using that knowledge as a springboard to design our ideal lives.

My aim is to provide that knowledge and confidence for you.

WRITING THIS BOOK

Messy. Challenging. Tiring. Relief. Grateful. Happy. I can use many other adjectives to describe the process of how this book came about. Dealing with the highs and lows of writing, rewriting, falling out of love with it, then falling back in love. In the early days, I was doing too much. In the later days, I was doing too little. Writing a book challenges and builds your resilience as you learn how to manage your motivation. Falling in love with a process and never losing sight of the end goal brings an indescribable joy when you succeed.

The idea for this book came in 2018 and 2019 as I began publishing articles on my website, blakedevos.com. I used my articles and research to educate myself and others on how we can usefully perform in our career and personal lives. I targeted topics around productivity, habits, goal-setting and better living. The more articles I wrote, the more I understood these subjects to be the crux of creating a rewarding life. Ironically for me, focusing on these topics improved my writing. Through blogging, I built a habit that still wakes me up excited each morning to write. The initial feeling of having no idea where to start was replaced with putting words on a page and seeing where they took me. It took a couple of years of researching, learning, unlearning and honing in on a style, but I've learned something invaluable. I learnt *how* to practise, ultimately improving my ability to become patient (with most things). With a mindset change, I acted on what I visualised. And here I am. My words, in the palm of your hand.

READING THIS BOOK

Some incredible and respectable authors, researchers and speakers have influenced not only my life but different concepts that appear throughout this book. My aim is not to reinvent the wheel, but to impart thoughts and encourage you to work towards your ideal life in the simplest way possible. The themes surrounding each pillar are shared with the intention to inspire your thoughts as you process this information, helping and motivating you to take action without looking back. You can expect to ask yourself questions—diving in and retrieving a new direction in life, or the same direction with improved performance.

There are six pillars to this book:

Pillar One: Understand Yourself provides you with a foundation, a starting point in creating a rewarding life. This first pillar helps identify what you currently do as an individual, drawing from the strengths and weaknesses you possess. It's a look into your thoughts, perceptions and emotions, and uncovers what's truly important to you.

Pillar Two: The Choices You Make brings to light the science behind your decision-making and the importance of making optimal decisions. This pillar explores an effective decision-making process that supports your direction so you can perform the behaviours that align with what's important to you—all while understanding the mechanics and mental shortcuts to become aware of.

Pillar Three: Achieve What You Seek is a practical approach towards a rewarding life. It's easy to visualise what you want to achieve, but sustaining the right actions and behaviours can be challenging to progress and succeed. Pillar three provides a practical pathway for continual achievement, which includes setting the right kind of goals and not getting caught up in the outcome.

Pillar Four: Develop Effective Habits explores the goals we set and the habits we need to create and implement to achieve those goals. Expect to go deep in aligning your practises with who you want to become while learning how to apply simple approaches to become that person.

Pillar Five: Optimal Performance provides an understanding of how you can continuously improve over time while achieving effective and consistent results. Your ability to perform well requires longevity in your actions. In this pillar, you'll learn how you can create more valuable time in your day and excel significantly in the areas you choose to focus on.

Pillar Six: Living In This World highlights how you can live a rewarding life when your direction meets with the unexpected. Some things we can control, but there are also uncontrollable situations that life brings. This pillar provides a solid case for you to prioritise your pursuits and not to put them on the back burner while trying to control the controllable. Instead, you'll learn to navigate your way through the curveball's life will inevitably throw you.

To alter our life for the better, we often believe we need to make brash, drastic changes. Because we're clouded by emotions, judgement, technology and wavering energy levels, we fail to recognise that it's the simplest strategies which help us. Where we fall short is in our awareness to learn what it takes to improve as opposed to how we think we will feel.

If there's just one takeaway I'd like you to get from this book, let it be your ability to take action and live a useful life. A life where you wake up each morning with continual energy, harnessing joy and experience. It's all within us—we just need to know where to look.

It's time to live a rewarding life.

PILLAR I

UNDERSTAND YOURSELF

"Dig deep within yourself, for there is a fountain of goodness ever ready to flow if you will keep digging". – Marcus Aurelius

Before you can apply actions and behaviours that produce an exceptional life, it's essential to acknowledge what you do, why you do it and how to act when presented with reactive triggers. Unconscious thoughts lead to unconscious actions. Awareness hones in on what becomes useful and what is useless as your attention shifts towards a rewarding life. The first pillar, Understand Yourself, forms the foundation to reveal your focus for belief in a world where it's possible to change the trajectory of your life.

You can act on a business idea.
You can advance in the career you love.
You can turn a hobby into a passion.
You can learn a new skill and become an expert.
You can write the book you've been thinking about.

So let's begin with a story.

Tommy Caldwell grew up in Loveland, Colorado. His father, Mike Caldwell, was a professional bodybuilder and rock climber who introduced Tommy to the sport at a young age. The Caldwell family took annual trips to Yosemite National Park, where Tommy first grew his love for rock climbing. In 1995, Tommy and his father drove to his first rock climbing event where he outlasted the other competitors in the contest. Whether through sheer shock or reward for winning the competition, the organisers extended Tommy an invitation to compete in the international rock climbing championship. Tommy accepted and the next day he climbed a one-hundred-and-twenty-foot, man-made wall to challenge for the championship. He was the only climber to reach the top and again beat all the other experienced climbers. From that moment on, Tommy gained notoriety as a young, up and coming climber. As he continued competing around the United States, Tommy met fellow climber Beth Rodden. Beth lived and breathed climbing, and the two became close very quickly.

In 2000, Tommy and Beth were invited to go climbing in Kyrgyzstan—a beautiful mountain country in Central Asia. Four climbers participated in the tour. They were chartered out by helicopter into the Kara-Su Valley. A week and a half into the trip a sequence of events began that would forever change their lives. As Tommy, Beth and the two other climbers lay in their hanging cot one thousand feet up the wall, they woke up to several loud bangs. "Oh my god, we're getting shot at!" Tommy screamed. The sound of gunshots rang out as bullets flew off the wall. With nowhere to go and frightened for their lives, Tommy and Beth looked below and saw a couple of small figures waving at them to come down. After the climbers fearfully made their way to the ground, four heavily armed men forced the climbers to walk back to their base camp. As they arrived, all of their tents had been cut open, belongings spread out in the meadow and food taken.

The armed men were known to be part of the Islamic Movement of Uzbekistan (IMU)—a rebel group who worked alongside Al-Qaeda and the Taliban. As the four climbers were surrounded, a firefight ensued. Kyrgyzstan Military soldiers began firing at the IMU, screaming at the climbers to hide from the rebels. One Kyrgyzstan military soldier made it close enough to Tommy and Beth but was executed right in front of the pair. As the gunfire died down, it started to get dark. The rebels marched Tommy, Beth and the other two climbers up through the Kara-Su Valley mountains.

The four rebels and four climbers hiked at eleven thousand feet elevation with no warm clothes or food. They hiked through the night and the rebels hid the climbers during the day, burying them in holes so they couldn't be detected by the military. The hiding and hiking went on for six days before the climbers realised the rebels had no plan. They were going in circles. Two captors had left a couple of days earlier to find food but were later found shot dead on the ground, presumably from the military. In a desperate bid to escape, the other two climbers, John and Jason, began plotting how they could outsmart the captors.

On the sixth day of captivity, the two remaining captors split up and began looking for food. One would go independently, and the other captor would walk with the climbers in another direction. Tommy, Beth, John and Jason were comfortable on the terrain. They noticed their captor having problems walking on such a rough surface. They thought that if they were going to escape, now was the time. John and Jason had communicated to Tommy and Beth that they would try to push the rebel off one of the cliff faces and attempt to run away. They looked for a point to push as their captor directed them to walk but couldn't find one. As they got to the peak of one of the mountains, Tommy realised their opportunity would be over. He decided that this was what he had to do to survive. Tommy said to Beth, "Do you think I should do this?" Beth didn't respond. She wasn't sure. Tommy turned towards his captor. He ran up behind him, grabbed his gun strap, placed one hand on his chest, and extended his arms out, sending him off the cliff. For Tommy, his decision was in the moment. Fight or flight. Kill or be killed.

Tommy broke down. He dropped to his knees, sobbing in panic. His world had come crashing down. But there was no time to weep. The adrenaline to escape kicked in for the climbers. They remembered passing a military base when they were hiking and ran towards the direction. Finally, after four hours of running through the darkness down the valley, they were greeted by a man waving his gun. They all put their hands in the air shouting, "We're Americans!" It was the Kyrgyz Army. The group had finally been rescued and were flown back to safety.

Upon return to America, the traumatic experience took a toll on Tommy. He started to become an entirely different person. After Kyrgyzstan, Tommy and Beth tried to absorb what had happened. They thought seeing a therapist and attending church together would resolve the changes they were experiencing. After a break from climbing, Tommy decided to get back on the wall. It was a place he found peace in his mind. For Tommy, climbing reminded him back to where it all began—a symbolic feeling in an attempt to enjoy his life after the experiences he had been through. The enjoyment and motivation pushed Tommy to start setting goals for himself. He mapped out more complex routes and focused on challenging himself to succeed in different climbs. Climbing was just like it used to be.

Life started to look up, and although Tommy and Beth still had their struggles processing their emotions and experiences, they did it together through climbing. But even after all they went through, Tommy's life was again about to change. One afternoon, Tommy and Beth were remodelling his parents' cabin and Tommy was using an old table saw. He tried to cut a small piece of wood but the blade caught, sucking Tommy's hand back in and completely slicing off his index finger. He screamed, "I fucking cut off my finger, I cut off my finger!" Tommy's finger lay in a pile of sawdust. A stunned Beth tried to remain calm while Tommy stood there in shock. She picked up the severed finger, placed it on ice and drove Tommy to the hospital.

For two weeks, surgeons tried to reattach his finger. After three surgeries, it became apparent the finger wasn't going to survive. One doctor, a fellow climber, came into the room and told Tommy he would have to find a new career. The doctor advised that it would be impossible to climb due to the nerve damage and loss of an index finger. Tommy disagreed. After surgery, he began to retrain the nerves in his hand. He started building confidence and with it came a reserve of energy never felt before. Tommy attempted a climb he failed at before cutting off his finger. But this time he succeeded, proving to himself and the surgeons that he could still accomplish great climbs, even with one finger missing.

High on confidence, Tommy started climbing other faces of El Capitan with Beth. Not long after, despite all they had been through, they got married and bought a property twenty minutes away from the area, with a plan to live their dream in Yosemite—a place where they would raise their kids and climb every day.

Unfortunately, in life, not everything goes as planned. In what seemed like a dream, cracks started to show in their relationship. Hostility towards each other became present and they began to grow apart. The love for climbing they shared wasn't enough to hold their relationship together anymore. Once they got divorced, Tommy was crushed. He went back to the one place he always found solace: climbing. The experience in Kyrgyzstan, the loss of his finger and the loss of his wife were all moments in Tommy's life he had to overcome. These adversities presented reactive triggers for Tommy to work through. He dealt with these triggers the only way he knew how. Over the next five years following the divorce, Tommy obsessively planned an ascent up the Dawn Wall. The wall, measuring a height of nine hundred and fourteen metres, had never been climbed before. The Dawn Wall has more hard pitches than any other route on El Capitan combined. Tommy believed he could do it, even with one less finger.

But if Tommy were to achieve the ascent, he needed a climbing partner. He found Kevin Jorgeson, a world-class boulderer from California, who had zero wall climbing experience. In their years of preparation, the two ventured into Yosemite, exploring individual pitches and how they would solve the seemingly impossible puzzle of the Dawn Wall. The remarkable patience of Tommy and Kevin's preparation for a climb of this magnitude was finally put on display. In 2015, they captivated the world as they set out to climb the Dawn Wall. They spent nineteen gruelling days up in the air, challenging their physical and mental resolve before finally making it to the top.

Of course, they were not without their struggles. Halfway through the climb, it looked as though Kevin would not make it past a critical pitch. Pitch fifteen, an incredibly technical section of the wall, required the pair to launch themselves and grab two of the smallest, sharpest holds of the rock face. Ten times Kevin tried, and ten times he failed. After each attempt, Kevin would spend the day recovering on their hanging base camp to let his fingers heal. Kevin urged Tommy to keep climbing up the wall without him, but Tommy refused and waited for his friend to succeed. After seven days and eleven attempts, Kevin stuck the landing. He could hear cheers from the camped-out media and onlookers from the ground who followed their every move up the wall. From there, the pair powered through the remaining sections.

After navigating nineteen days on the wall and finally making it to the top, Tommy and Kevin attracted global media attention. The Dawn Wall took seven years of planning, training and strategizing. It was only supposed to take as long as twelve days to complete, but the perseverance and patience on pitch fifteen led to the pair achieving the most extraordinary feat in climbing history. In an interview Jorgeson said, "That is the most pressure I've been under. Sometimes you have to put yourself in a position to fail or in a position to experience so much pressure to discover what you're capable of".

As for Tommy, he now lives a rewarding and full life. Climbing taught him to live without fear and to practise the act of courage. The traumatic experience in Kyrgyzstan was his greatest hardship. Recovering from the trauma helped Tommy become a much stronger and life-loving individual. He is now a devoted father and husband, and he shares his story and love for life and climbing with anyone who will listen.

After the series of adversities he faced, including a fight for survival, why did Tommy continue on the path of climbing? Why did Kevin Jorgeson persevere and continue his way to the top of the Dawn Wall after failing pitch fifteen seven days in a row? Was it the fear of letting themselves or their family and friends down? Was it the pressure of a society where failing is not an option? Or was it simply to achieve something great?

Even if we put ourselves in their shoes, we may not truly grasp an accurate understanding. But what we can and should identify is how Tommy's story of consistent adversity and triumphs represent the unrelenting elements of life we go through. In some form, we all experience basic emotions: fear, happiness, resilience, love, sadness, heartbreak and success. How you respond will ultimately determine the trajectory of your outcomes.

The challenges you face, whether in the workplace or at home, may not be as punishing as what life threw at Tommy. But Tommy's story teaches us to recognise our abilities and encourages us to pursue what we seek. It's a reminder for us to embrace the necessary and unnecessary struggles that align with what it takes to build a rewarding life. We should recognise that patience and process involve both overcoming adversities and following what's important to us.

It doesn't matter if you're a full-time worker, a writer, an entrepreneur or a student. There are internal and external components which constitute your actions.

It's crucial to understand how you react to your emotions and to change, and it's essential to notice what you consume and the lifestyle you live. Understanding Yourself provides awareness and clarity in what it is you seek.

What stands in your way? Who do you want to become? Who do you want by your side?

There are common misconceptions of what it takes to create a rewarding life. We think:

- We need more money.
- The timing needs to be right.
- We haven't gained the right skills.
- Comfort and security trumps discomfort and insecurities.

We don't intend on these being excuses because what we think is how we perceive our own unique situation. But the reality is that we become limited in this way of thinking. Engaging in this type of self-talk limits the actions and direction we take because we aren't fully aware of what is possible. There's no alignment in our thoughts and pursuing fulfilment.

To begin living a rewarding life, we're required to look into what we value and connect it to our reality. And to achieve this, we need to get to know our egos.

1

CHECK YOUR EGO

Now is the time to think about what's important in your life. Why do you do what you do? Who do you do it for? We often waste precious time doing things we don't enjoy in order to prove ourselves to people who don't care. As individuals, we attempt to be better and more than ourselves and others. For example, we excel in a job because we've worked hard to get to the top, but then we continue to complain because not everything's on our terms. Or, when starting a new venture, we tend to focus on the validation of building something new rather than creating a product or service that becomes great. We have ambition but are out of touch with reality, creating unrealistic expectations and requirements for ourselves. That's our ego at play.

In its simplest form, ego is how we view our own importance. We all have beliefs, values, behaviours and habits that make up our personalities and unconscious mind. Whenever our identity is challenged, our ego is there to defend us. We use it to protect ourselves in various ways: we refuse help, we consistently compare ourselves to others, we reject new ideas and we believe what we see is clear-cut with no room for new thoughts. The most basic example of ego is clear in political debates. Those who are debating do not change their own minds, and they do not change their opponent's mind either. They defend their beliefs and project their ideas to you and me, and how we approve or reject the debate is tied to our identity and previous experiences.

Ego provides us with conflicting opinions, and it often comes from a place of anger because we feel out of control when challenged.

But our ego shouldn't be something we hold back. That would mean we don't see ourselves as important. It should be something we learn to control and acknowledge. We have a choice in life: to be someone remarkable or to do something remarkable. When we attempt to be someone remarkable, we take shortcuts, willing to sacrifice our beliefs and values to succeed. Instead of possessing humility and purpose, we take more for ourselves and keep it close instead of sharing it with those that matter. When we choose to do something remarkable, we're driven by purpose and process. We are less worried about credit and recognition, and our rewards are motivating. We don't seek validation when it's all said and done. Because it's never said and done.

Your ego will always be there. It works to assemble your personality and manage your identity while protecting you from societal expectations. Why? Because you're expected to perform at your best. We only have to look as far as the classroom to see its effect. Teachers seek brilliant results from students and students seek valuable learning from teachers.

We rarely examine our ego, but maybe it's time we should.

When the global COVID-19 pandemic arrived, the crisis upended businesses and forced organisational leaders to pivot. The pandemic demanded adaptation to a more virtual way of operating and living. Companies had to keep themselves afloat. Many struggled with changes at home and processing the emotions of being unable to see family, being confined to a house and being told what freedoms they had and did not have. Of course, there was anger, sadness and frustration. Having your freedoms taken away contradicted basic human rights—it's human nature to feel a certain type of way. But while we felt like we lost plenty, it was also a time for us to check our egos.

When we focus solely on ourselves and our own opinions, we miss the opportunity to improve other areas of our lives. Post-pandemic, employees remembered if their leaders responded with humility or ego. It determined whether an organisation improved its culture or disconnected with its staff. As individuals, it was a time for us to check in on friends and family a lot more than we would. It gave us a chance to try something new or to improve our knowledge, which we wouldn't have thought to do otherwise.

The problem our ego brings is when our self-importance overshadows our sense of purpose through altering stages of our life. When we reject the ability to create and grow and we lose sight of what we truly love, our ego takes control. It's why we saw people change career paths during the pandemic. Some transitioned into virtual careers, while others realised how much they relied on colleagues to get them through the work week. One of the greatest tests of the crisis was to reflect on what we were trying to achieve and discover if it was in line with who we are and what we value.

For all of us, there comes a time not only when we must reflect on our direction and where our success comes from but on how we live as well.

Ask yourself this question: is what I'm doing sustainable?

We often believe successful individuals earn their success through consistent high energy and constant enthusiasm. Their ego gets excused because we believe it's how they made it to the top. While ego may have gotten them to where they are, will it last forever? We see professional athletes possess these traits. They believe they will beat any opponent on any day. It's rare to find an athlete who doesn't want to get to the top or win the championship as fast as possible. They convince themselves that ego and energy are the only way to stay there. But what happens once the athlete retires?

It's not just the athlete. What happens if an entrepreneur

loses it all? And what about the confident writer who continually gets rejected? What happens to their ego? It either hits them hard or they have been preparing silently through humility and purpose. And if it's the latter—they have been attempting to do something great. They don't prepare for *if*, but *when* success happens, and they do so by projecting their own self-importance on doing, not being.

At some point, you've experienced your own ego taking control, likely while someone projected their ego on you. For example, when working for a company, managers set the tone early with their newly employed staff member. They communicate their expectations on what they should and shouldn't do. The employee is then left to navigate their way through office politics, where it becomes apparent to other colleagues if they can work with that person. The hierarchy of organisations promotes the stroking of ego.

Should it be this way? No. But is it often the case? Yes.

Far too often, we experience our own or someone else's ego projected on us, which becomes detrimental to our ability to gain confidence, learn and pursue challenging situations with the right intent. Albert Einstein said, "More the knowledge, lesser the ego. Lesser the knowledge, more the ego". We can't remove ego because we're always learning. We should, however, remain vigilant in how it's projected and keep it quiet. If ego were to be killed, we wouldn't have aspirations. There would be no direction and purpose because confidence is lost. Without an ego, we don't believe we're important. But to live a life as good as you want, you need to value what you do and who you do it for. You have to believe that you're necessary and what you do is of worth.

To continue practising and preparing, you must accept, believe, learn and build confidence. The key is to remember that applying consistent effort in the areas you value, while practising humility in a world of chaos, keeps your ego quiet and your confidence high. Your ego is not there to be killed but to be nurtured and to coexist with your awareness.

Will you awaken your ego and be someone remarkable merely through validation? Or will you do something remarkable by leveraging your ego for energy and growth? Just remember this: If you put your ego in the passenger seat, you become more aware of the conditions in which you drive your life. But if you let ego take the wheel, you lose humility and awareness to do something remarkable. You can write the book you have been putting off. You can change careers if it's no longer serving you. You can make a positive impact on many lives.

As legendary Arsenal defender Tony Adams once said, "Play for the name on the front of your jersey, and they will remember the name on the back".

Focus on the value of what you do and who you do it for, then you won't have to worry about validation and achievement —they take care of themselves.

2

APPRECIATE YOUR EMOTIONS

Following the heinous terror attacks on September 11, 2001, millions of Americans stopped travelling by plane across the United States. When air travel decreased, car travel increased. Studies found that Americans opted to drive long distances instead of a shorter flight.[1] Not considering 9/11, in 2001, there were 331 aeroplane crash fatalities in the US from 1,751 crash events. On the road, there were 42,000 driving-related deaths in that same year. Statistics imply that post 9/11, Americans were more willing to risk mortality in long-distance car travel rather than adopt the safer air travel option.[1] It's safe to assume the public's perception of risk from terrorism threats led to more driving-related deaths. It's also possible the September 11 terrorist attacks may have resulted in a secondary toll of deaths because people made poor choices to avoid imagined scenarios of risk.[2]

As humans, we believe it's sensible to make irrational decisions so we can avoid fearful emotions. History tells us that any large-scale threat to public safety affects the emotions and decisions we make. The world has experienced many events that have affected our lives and how we respond, with no end to these events in sight. To build a rewarding life, and one with conviction, we're required to have an understanding of sensibility. We need to learn and experience what it's like to *feel* in different ways as we continue to create our ideal world.

Emotions are powerful feelings derived from mood, circumstance or relationship with others. Emotions are expressed through psychological functions such as facial expressions, a faster heartbeat or a specific behaviour. Through the limbic system, our emotional experiences develop as pleasant or unpleasant mental states. The limbic system is a group of brain structures that act as a control centre for conscious and unconscious functions. In some ways, the limbic system connects the mind and body to close the gap between psychological and physiological experiences. One way this function occurs is when a fight-or-flight response is activated. The limbic system triggers a physical reaction to an emotional experience. This system helps our bodies respond to the intense emotions we have.

Your emotional responses are a reaction to your current environment.

You're supposed to smile at a baby because it's our evolutionary advantage to give infants positive emotions.

You're supposed to react with a fight-or-flight response under perceived danger because self-preservation is part of our DNA.

What we rarely think of are the thousands of micro reactions we face every day. You've likely experienced a time when the waiter at a restaurant is polite, so you respond with kindness. Or a car cuts you off, so you abuse them. While many emotional expressions are universal, there are sociocultural norms that dictate how we respond when coming across an intense emotion. For example, in Japan people tend to hide their display of fear or disapproval when an authoritative figure is present.

Conversely, in western cultures people are more likely to express their negative emotions amongst others.[3]

When we experience an intense emotion, instead of ignoring it, we can control it and use it to make the world a better place. Climate change, domestic abuse, racial injustice and human trafficking are all relevant issues in today's society. Unfortunately, many of our efforts to deal with social and cultural issues involve expressing intense emotions through anger and frustration, leading to emotional stress and poor mental well-being. The adverse reaction we may feel about these issues can be used more positively by donating our time, helping others or educating ourselves and those around us.

When you show emotion, you're putting a meaningful stamp on your experiences. They're a key driver in our behaviour and shape our responses to our environments. Emotions enable you to decide, take action, connect, communicate and build meaningful friendships and relationships with others. While it's good to understand how we feel, it's equally important to understand and recognise the emotional behaviour in others. If we can implement empathy, we're better at channelling our behaviours in a positive way. Empathy creates two things: self-awareness and calculated, responsive behaviours. When we showcase these traits, we have more strength and willingness to make intuitive decisions.

Unfortunately, we're often told not to "get too emotional". When women show emotion, they're perceived as showing "too much" or "overreacting". On the flip side, when men show emotion, they're perceived as "weak". Many of us feel a multitude of emotions in a single day. Some emotions help us and others don't. For instance, joy, gratitude and courage provide us with positive experiences, but worry, obligation and jealousy have the potential to impart unnecessary emotional energy.

Feelings are subjective, meaning uncommon events can evoke different emotions. Our reactions are related to our background, experiences and personality. For example, public speaking may be enjoyable for some, but it can trigger acute anxiety and stress for others. When you're more aware of your emotional state, you're better at reading the emotional state of others.

Neuroscientist Joseph LeDoux has influenced much of our understanding of the purpose and origins of emotions. LeDoux explains that our emotional responses become hardwired into our brain, where emotions trigger an instinctive reaction without the need for conscious thought.[4] What we can take away from this finding is that our emotions involve a change to both our physical and mental state. The most obvious signs of a physical response to a mental state is an increased heart rate when stressed and tightening in the chest when fatigued.

When faced with a big decision, do you decide based on the emotions you currently feel and your gut instinct, or do you weigh up the pros and cons?

Decision-making is one of the most important aspects to master in all facets of life.

Following your intuition can be a great way to tap into your beliefs and values, but even when we weigh our options, we're still emotional beings.

Consider this question: what do you believe is most needed to make optimal, well-informed decisions from the list below?

- Your ability to think clearly
- The gathering of all the facts
- Assessing all risks
- Not letting emotion get in the way of a decision

Which would you choose? When making decisions, the expected solution is to leave emotion out of the equation. We're told only to use logic and that will create the best choice. But all decisions you make are, at the core, based on emotion. For example:

- The decision to have children bases itself on joy and love.

- Deciding to change careers represents emotional thoughts of what our future looks like.
- The decision to award a new contract has an emotional attachment to the company because they want to be seen and earn money.

In his book *Descartes' Error*, neuroscientist Antonio Damasio describes Elliot, one of his high-profile cases. Elliot was a successful businessman, husband and father. He unfortunately had a tumour in his frontal lobe and undertook surgery for the removal. Following the operation, Elliot reported to Damasio that his life had broken down. He didn't know how to live anymore. His marriage fell apart, as did every new business venture he started. What's interesting is Elliot was still in the ninety-seventh percentile for IQ but no longer had any motivation. Damasio found Elliot to be a man void of emotion. A man who emerged as a human with normal intellect, but unable to make any decisions that were presented to him.

To have direction and purpose in anything you do, you're required to feel and have emotion. To put it simply: Emotion motivates us to either continue or cease.

When we describe someone as emotional, we often assume they lack good judgement. But emotions enable us to weigh up options and find the best outcome for ourselves—a vital component in our decision-making process. When deciding, we look for a way to satisfy basic human needs. It's why many choices we make are unconscious attempts to avoid guilt, fear and negative feelings. We do this while simultaneously attempting to enhance our positive emotions—much like choosing to travel by car to avoid the risk of a terror threat in the air.

The relationship between the decisions you make and the emotions you convey means quick choices are often based on how you feel, where you associate a new feeling with the decision you have just created. For example, you might have had a stressful day at work. You skipped lunch and ended up ordering fast food on the way home. The quick decision to order fast food means you forgot dinner was waiting for you in the fridge.

The powerful influence our emotions have over our thought processes means our decisions are susceptible to error. And because we value our time, decisions are often fast and automatic so we can feel a certain way for as long as possible. We rarely realise the full impact of emotional interference in our decisions.

Your emotions are there for a reason. They're the rudder of your ship that helps navigate you through calm and rough seas. Understanding what you feel not only spares you from unexpected breakdowns but guides you towards creating a happier self and living a more useful life.

It's important we engage with people from this perspective. We should show empathy, read the emotions in their faces and show them we're listening and paying attention, practise kindness and expect nothing in return. Through the avenue of understanding and acknowledging your feelings and reactions, you can build resilience and a motivation to pursue what you seek and help others do the same.

3

CHANGE AND NEW EXPERIENCES

Your life is subject to change at any moment. The community you are part of, the society you live in and the organisations you work for are all affected by ripples of change. Change directly and indirectly impacts what you feel and how you act. The changes you go through can be a result of your own doing, or they can be scenarios beyond your control. Unfortunately, we rarely reciprocate well when our circumstances alter because we find comfort in our habits and what is familiar to us.

Even when deciding to make changes within ourselves, when confronted with this change, the new and improved transition can prove a challenging adjustment. We naturally resist because we're confronted with uncertainty. Our brain feels the uncertain pressure of change because it wants to keep us alive and safe. Although change is not necessarily life-threatening, the brain has wired itself to function that way. It plays a regular role in how we as individuals live through the different aspects of our lives. For example:

- We avoid a career change because of the fear of starting over again.
- We struggle to accept a reduction in income because our ego says we're going backwards.

- We don't learn a new skill or take up a new hobby because it's easier to go through the motions of what we currently do.
- We count down the days to retirement because it's preferable to the perceived risk of failing when pivoting to something we enjoy.
- We resist going to the gym and hiring a personal trainer because of the anxiety it brings.
- We fill our minds with excuses, tension and nervousness, causing us not to act on how we feel about the person we care about.

While change seems and feels terrifying, it shouldn't be allowed to trap us into living stagnant lives. The real calamity is living a life that brings little joy.

The activities you carry out each day come from an area of the brain which plays a significant role in forming long-standing habits. When performing unconscious behaviours, you exert much less energy because the circuits employed have already been shaped and defined through your previous experiences. For instance, brushing your teeth, making a coffee each morning or driving to work are all subconscious examples of things you automatically do.

When activities are engaged in this form, it frees up a part of the brain to focus on fresh and new inputs. Once a routine becomes wired into your brain, whether it's healthy or unhealthy, it makes it hard for your brain to override and make a change. Although bad habits often remain, it is possible to replace them over time with new, more effective habits that align with your direction.

We're all reminded of the benefits of having a strong routine, but we aren't so aware that routines require consistent updating. Olympian boxer Harry Garside makes changes to his routine each month, putting himself in a position to test his responses to change and embrace resistant barriers. At the 2020 Tokyo Olympics, Garside challenged himself not to talk for seventy-two hours as soon as he arrived. He told his team the only time he would talk would be to say yes or no during sparring with his coach.[1] Garside also started ballet, which significantly improved his boxing. The boxer ended up winning a Bronze medal at the Tokyo 2020 Olympics, marking the first time in three decades an Australian won an Olympic boxing medal.

In an interview with an Australian radio presenter, Garside said, "Each challenge teaches me something new and it makes me understand more things about myself. I'm learning to love every bit about myself. I'm trying to push myself in every way, shape or form".

Putting himself in challenging situations has become his monthly routine. He continues to create different avenues that exploit his performance as an athlete and a human being, and this approach has resulted in a rewarding life.

Most of us do the comfortable things well, and it's easy in those moments to feel we don't need to change. But for many of us, switching up our routine not only forces us to pay more attention to what we're doing, but it also changes our habitual behaviours—exposing us to a new set of triggers.

When you use changes in routine to your advantage, your improvements compound over time.

Life changes are inevitable and can be both enjoyable and unpleasant. But it's often the case that the small changes make life more interesting. For instance, we might try a different sport, change our diet or visit a new local restaurant. These changes are often easy to accept because they aren't permanently embedded in our identity. When there's development in something new, our experiences alter. We can gain new friends, new skills or a new confidence in life. Change is essential for development and growth. Without it, we assure ourselves of staying in the same monotonous routine, going through the same motions and dwelling on the same feelings.

Our lives don't get better by chance—they get better by our actions. Change comes into our lives because of probability, crisis or choice. We force ourselves to weigh up our options and decide if we change any situation. What stops us from learning and growing is being unprepared and resistant. When we keep ourselves from accepting something new, we rob ourselves of a choice or control over how we want to live. Life becomes reactionary and we're continually one step behind reality. Although we're unable to control unexpected events like death, loss of employment or illness, these events challenge us, remind us and give us opportunities to focus on what we can control. If we ignore the challenge of change, we deny the opportunity and ability to live effectively.

What we focus on determines the direction we take. We know that what we focus on expands and becomes more important than what we put in the back of our minds. Because of the brain's proclivity to implement habits, repetitions of deliberate action yield conditioned responses to experiences that form our lives by default. When going through a process of change, stepping into the unknown is a prerequisite to building new behaviour patterns. It's necessary to consider yourself a student of change who gains new experiences.

It's often the case when starting something new that we try to get everything right the first time. When I first started writing, I thought I had to write the perfect article, create the perfect style and have the best software. Initially it paralysed my work because I was focusing on everything being 100%. It wasn't until I started to focus on the 1% that things started to change (more about this later).

When starting something new, you need to ensure it comes from a place of self-compassion instead of self-criticism. Expecting mistakes is a valuable thought to have because it saves us from perfectionism and opens up a newly found creative route.

4
ALL WE CONSUME

Humans have an uncanny ability to transform their environment. We've seen significant improvements over the last fifty years in how we live and communicate with others. Even living through a pandemic, our lives initially turned upside down and we were forced to adapt. Our drive for change and adaptation has accelerated with more advancements thrown our way. We are constantly innovating to meet demands and succeed in the way we live, and we don't want to be left behind.

Unfortunately, the same society we adapt to is limited in its ability to consume all that's thrown our way. The world around us is constantly changing, but we remain imperfect social and emotional humans. The brain's primary role is to keep us alive and functioning, but we continually struggle with excessive consumption. You and I don't have the brainpower to deal with all the stimulus we receive. And, while every innovation and advancement in technology is supposed to give us greater productivity and efficiency, it comes at a cost. Distractions are more apparent than ever. Society demands that we be responsive, productive, make quick decisions and seek immediate rewards. We're encouraged by family, friends and acquaintances to excel in everything we do. Unfortunately, with so much information in our lives, we deny ourselves the time and space to slow down, take a step back and take action on the life we visualise.

Wherever you look, there's technology. Over the years, technology has transformed the way we act, think, communicate and live. Think how accustomed you are to instant information and real-time feedback. In today's world, if a page doesn't load within the first five seconds, you move on to the next. If your food takes a long time at a restaurant, your patience wears thin. All these micro-behaviours you perform throughout the day are rarely conscious thoughts. More of us are finding a potential partner by the swipe of a screen because it's a lot easier to connect with someone. We read, watch movies, order food and purchase items all through a touch of a button. Speedy responses and faster results are defining us at an increasing rate. And the reason? In today's environment, we seek and demand immediacy.

It's hard to imagine a life without a search engine where we have direct access to answers to our questions. A lot of what we do today is surrounded by technology.

For example, we join social media groups that provide us with advice on living a rewarding life, but the addictive nature of technology can force us to rely solely on the advice of others. When this occurs, the potential of inaction and comparing ourselves to others increases because we're receiving different advice from different individuals—potentially paralysing our decision-making.

While it's wonderful to manage our time, exchange information and shape our opinions through technology, there is a downside. We can become a prisoner to a virtual network that can then validate, endorse or demean our identity. We only need to look at the impact bullying has through social media platforms. Teenagers and adults are continually subjected to words, memes and other forms of online bullying that can have long-lasting effects.

A virtual network can shape our identity and success, yes,

but it can also destroy it. What you consume has the ability to derail your progress. For instance:

- Professional athletes are consistently subject to criticism in the public eye as they attempt to evolve their skillset.
- Politicians are under a microscope in any decisions they make but use social media to provide resolutions to concerned members of the public.
- Influencers are criticised for their savvy ability to sell products and promote themselves online but have built a like-minded and safe community with others.

While our criticism at times can be valid, as a society we consistently overstep the mark and forget they, too, are human and our criticism is not of importance. We get caught up in destructive condemnation because it's easy. Before communicating virtually, we need to stop and ask ourselves, is what I'm consuming important to me? Our answer ultimately determines whether our time is better spent elsewhere or if we can gain something valuable from engaging.

The internet is governed by social opinion, followers and relationships that often won't last without a network. As the evolution of technology continues to create more platforms, we need to become more aware of the environment we surround ourselves in and understand the costs associated with what we consume. The good news is that we can develop awareness and implement strategies and techniques that lead a more effective life. While your agenda is different from the next person, we all seek something universal: listening to our intuition, pursuing what we seek and creating our ideal reality. The common denominator in human beings, regardless of where we come from, is our ability to work through pain and suffering and be happy and filled with life. The way to achieve this is entirely dependent on ourselves.

Become more aware by paying attention to what you truly value. Shift your focus towards your ideal reality by asking yourself the right questions. Instead of asking yourself why you feel stuck, ask, what is my next best move forward? Or, if you always question why you give up easily, reframe that thought by asking, what do I want to accomplish? Introspection is a powerful tool that is available to use whenever we seek awareness and understanding of our own insights and behaviour.

MAINTAIN A BALANCED ENVIRONMENT

In modern-day society, the definition of the word "lifestyle" is contentious. Alfred Adler first introduced the term in his 1929 book *The Case of Miss R.* where he defined the word as "a person's basic character, established early in childhood". Since then, lifestyle has adapted a broader meaning, currently interpreted as "the way we live". For us as individuals, our lifestyle reflects our attitudes, beliefs and worldview. We forge a sense of self and create norms that represent our identity. Even if the word is contentious, we can all agree on one thing: we live in different cultures and uphold different values but still want to live best in the environment we're in.

As the world speeds up around us, day-to-day living has somewhat been compromised. Many of us are forgoing our long-term health in exchange for less sleep, long working hours, poor diet and no exercise. We often choose to focus solely on only one part of our life to progress rather than taking a more balanced approach, ultimately leading to a decline in our well-being and self-care. Imagine someone who focuses heavily on their career. They work twelve-hour days sitting in an office, only to come home stressed and unable to switch off. They don't have time to exercise, never get a good night's sleep and they have poor eating habits. Over time, the effect builds up, leading to burnout and an inability to maintain sound mental energy. In the short term, their career is excelling. They meet deadlines with countless overtime hours and a promotion that's just around the corner. Although career-focused, how sustainable does this become in living up to their employers' expectations? If they get the promotion, will they have more responsibility requiring even longer hours? You would think so. Long term, the mental energy endured in the fast-paced, sedentary lifestyle catches up. Their mental health and physical health becomes compromised and their ability to function effectively is limited.

Meanwhile, their spouse is raising a newborn at home, striving to meet the demands of being a parent and a spouse. They feel like their partner consistently misses out on the opportunity to connect each evening, resulting in an ever-increasing strain to synchronise as a family. When the weekend comes, the working spouse would love nothing more than to switch off, but becomes frustrated every time the baby cries. Their emotions are heightened, and they struggle to cope. The cycle repeats, and because of an imbalanced lifestyle, the eventual result brings disconnect, leading to resentment and further emotional turmoil. What has ultimately occurred represents a dedicated and career-driven individual willing to financially support their family but later regrets not being fully present as a parent and spouse.

You may or may not be a parent, but it's important to underline our capacity to exist in an environment where lifestyle matters. You express your lifestyle through your behaviour, work, social patterns and leisure. What you do determines how you live. If you're unable to take control of your well-being, it makes it difficult to be available for others. While we have our commitments which require a significant amount of our time and resources, we should become more aware of the areas of our lifestyle which need to be managed and where we can improve.

Think about the behaviours you perform and assess if they're compromising who you want to be. Instead of focusing on the behaviour itself and removing it, spend your energy in other areas that are currently working and enhance those areas. Sometimes the solutions to your negative behaviours lie in other areas of your life which are still waiting to be complemented. If your good habits are strong, your bad habits become easier to unlearn and leave behind. Habits are a fundamental area to understand when creating a rewarding life, which we'll explore later in the book.

5

THE ANTIDOTE TO FEAR

In 1965, Jo was born in a small town near Bristol, England. Her father was an aircraft engineer at the Rolls Royce factory, and her mother, Anne, a science technician at a local school. Anne was diagnosed with Multiple Sclerosis when Jo was a teenager and died in 1990. When Jo was young, she surrounded herself with books and her classmates considered her the stereotypical bookworm with freckles and glasses.

From a young age, Jo wanted to be a writer. She wrote her first story at the age of six, a story about a rabbit. As she got older, Jo became a student at the University of Exeter in the UK where she studied French and the classics. She completed her degree and moved to London, working a series of jobs, including research at Amnesty International, a nonprofit organisation focusing on human rights. She continued scribbling on her notepad, creating more short stories. In 1990, Jo was on a delayed train from Manchester to London. She came up with the idea that would one day change her life. She began mapping out her notes in longhand and slowly built up a significant collection of papers which she took great care of.

Jo took her notes with her to Northern Portugal, where she taught English as a foreign language. She met and married Jorge in 1992, and the following year, their daughter Jessica was born.

Sadly, Jo's marriage didn't last long, ending in 1993. Jo decided she would finish teaching in Northern Portugal and move back to the UK to live in Edinburgh, Scotland. She took just three things with her when she left: her daughter, her suitcase and her collection of notes. Arriving in Edinburgh, she began experiencing an incredibly deep fear for the first time. Her marriage had failed after just one year, she'd suffered a miscarriage, she was jobless and the relationship with her father was in tatters. Living in Edinburgh, Jo made ends meet by living off welfare as she took care of her five-month-old daughter.

Her fear and perceived failures led Jo to clinical depression and the verge of suicide. She eventually began writing the manuscript for her first novel, putting together her collection of notes she began writing in 1990. In 1995, Jo finished her first manuscript for her book *Harry Potter and The Philosopher's Stone*. She submitted the synopsis to book agents, and all twelve came back with rejection letters. Many UK publishers viewed the book as too long or they found the setting of a boarding school was "too exclusive" to readers. It wasn't until a small publisher, Bloomsbury's editorial team, gained interest in the manuscript that something changed. The submission was eventually accepted because the Bloomsbury director's eight-year-old daughter read a chapter and demanded to read the rest of the manuscript. It was eventually published in the UK in 1997 by Bloomsbury, under the pen name JK Rowling.

The book was an instant success, making Jo a prominent author overnight. She was thrown into a world she didn't know nor prepare for, but arrived at because she overcame her fears of failing as a mother and not being able to provide for her daughter. Since her first book was published, Harry Potter became the best-selling book series of all time, and Jo became the first billionaire author. Off the back of the book's success, high grossing films and plays were created, cementing the series further as one of the greatest franchises and stories of all time.

In an interview at the height of Rowling's success, she said, "I stopped pretending to myself that I was anything other than what I was and began to direct all my energy into finishing the only work that mattered to me. Had I really succeeded at anything else, I might never have found the determination to succeed in the one arena I believed I truly belonged. I was set free because my greatest fear had been realised, and I was still alive, and I still had a daughter whom I adored, and I had an old typewriter and a big idea. And so rock bottom became the solid foundation on which I rebuilt my life."[1]

Although much has been discovered on the brain's mechanisms associated with fear, there is far less known about the relationship courage plays. How does the brain decipher courage in real-life fearful situations that demand an immediate response? Researchers Dr. Yadin Dudai and Uri Nili devised an experimental paradigm where participants had to choose to advance an object closer or farther away while placed in an MRI machine. The objects were either a toy bear or a live snake. Prior to the study, participants were classified as fearful or fearless, depending on how they responded to the pre-participation questionnaire. In this instance, subjective fear of the participants refers to how they perceive their own fears. It's safe to assume that many of us are fearful of snakes.

As expected, the researchers observed that both high subjective fear and the manifestation of anxiety triggered the participants to move the snake farther away.

However, interestingly enough, participants who brought the snake closer appeared to have a high anxiety response but low subjective fear, and vice versa. The brain area that stood out to researchers was the subgenual anterior cingulate cortex (sgACC). This area was active only when courage was on display but quiet when fear took over. Surprisingly, when the sgACC increased, bodily indicators of fear reduced. Dudai and Nili agreed that if humans can stimulate or activate this brain region, we could go a long way into overcoming our fears.[2]

Courage does not come when we completely remove fear, but when we overcome it enough to act. A firefighter going into a burning house should display courage, but they are not fearless. A lifeguard swimming out to save someone caught in a rip should display courage, but again, they are not fearless. It's the repetition in their profession that has given them courage, confidence and character. Aristotle believed courage to be the most important quality in a human. He wrote, "Courage is the first of human virtues because it makes all others possible". Ernest Hemingway described courage as "grace under pressure".

We can create our own courage through consistency and effort, manufacturing our own experiences and giving us more ammunition to act.

To build a courageous character, we should regularly strengthen the muscle of courage. A mother and father might practise courage by choosing to parent in a way that is authentic to them. An aspiring author practises courage by producing and sharing work in the face of criticism. An athlete applies courage by staying positive and working harder after being benched.

How you build a courageous character starts with recognising the opportunity to act on your fears and anxiety. When you acknowledge your fears, you allow yourself to be put in a situation of discomfort. But this is where the magic happens. Through discomfort, your perspective on your fears begins to change, and what you previously considered frightening and fearful turns into something much more rewarding and valuable. Rather than saying, "I don't think I can overcome this fear," reframe the question and ask, "What courageous action can I practise?" Your ability to face and overcome fears requires the powerful antidote of courageous practise. One act of courage does not remove fear—it's the acts of consistency which manage it.

6

START TO LIVE

Known as a successful businessman, Galen Litchfield was based in China in 1942 when the Japanese invaded. Shortly after the Japanese took Pearl Harbour, the military swarmed Shanghai, where they would eventually run into the businessman. Litchfield was a manager of an insurance company. They stormed his workplace, ordering Litchfield to liquidate all of the company's assets. He had no choice in the matter. The admiral advised him to cooperate or he would face certain death.

Litchfield did as asked, liquidating all the assets for fear of his life. But there was one block of securities worth seven hundred and fifty thousand dollars which he left off the liquidating list. The security belonged to Hong Kong and was therefore not part of the Shanghai assets. After realising he should have liquidated all of the assets, Litchfield's stomach began to churn. He started to stress about what would happen if the Japanese found out about the seven hundred and fifty thousand dollar security.

It wasn't long until they did find out. The admiral stormed the insurance company, where luckily Litchfield wasn't present. The admiral told the head accountant that Litchfield defied the orders of the Japanese Army. During the Second Sino Japanese War, going against the Japanese military meant being sent to

Bridge House, a Shanghai prison controlled by the Japanese. Litchfield had friends who killed themselves before being transported to Bridge House and other friends who were killed within ten days of their stint from the questioning and torture.

Word got around and a frightened Litchfield heard the fearful news—the Japanese knew about the securities he left off. It was a Sunday afternoon and while sitting in his chair at home, he began figuring out his next steps. The good news was, Litchfield already had a technique for solving problems that worried him. For years, whenever a cloud of confusion and stress surrounded him, he would go to his typewriter and write out two questions:

1. What am I worried about?
2. What can I do about it?

When asking himself these questions, he gained clarity about his situation. Similar to how you might write down your goals, Litchfield wrote down his worries. The answer to the first question was easy. But the second question required more time with his thoughts, where eventually he came up with four options.

He wrote:

Question 1: What am I worried about?
"I am afraid I will be thrown into the Bridge House tomorrow morning".

Question 2: What can I do about it?
"I can try to explain to the Japanese admiral. But he doesn't speak English. If I try to explain to him through an interpreter, I may stir him up again. That might mean death, for he is cruel, and would instead dump me in the Bridge House than bother talking about it."

"I can try to escape. Impossible. They keep track of me all the time. I have to check in and out of my room at the YMCA. If I try to escape, I'll probably be captured and shot."

"I can stay here in my room and not go near the office again. If I do, the Japanese admiral will be suspicious. He will probably send soldiers to get me and throw me into the Bridge House without giving me a chance to say a word."

"I can go down to the office as usual on Monday morning. If I do, there is a chance that the Japanese admiral may be so busy that he will not think of what I did. Even if he does think of it, he may have cooled off and not bother me. If this happens, I am all right. Even if he does bother me, I'll still have a chance to try and explain what happened. So, going to the office as usual on Monday morning and acting as if nothing went wrong gives me two chances to escape the Bridge House".

Litchfield went with option four and arrived at the office as would be his normal routine. When he entered the office, he sat down at his desk and looked over at the admiral. Sitting down, smoking his cigarette, the admiral glared across the room but said nothing. Six weeks later, he left and went back to Tokyo. Litchfield's worries had ended and he could continue living life on his terms. Interestingly enough, 50% of his worries vanished when he arrived at a clear, definite decision and another 40% disappeared once he carried out his decision.

When three doctors told Earl P. Haney he had fatal duodenal ulcers, the outlook was gloomy. The doctors told him he didn't have long to live and advised him to rest and watch what he ate. After analysing the facts, Haney embraced his fate. After receiving the doctor's advice, Haney wrote out his will and bought a casket so his body could be shipped back to his family in Nebraska. He then began to travel the world, eat international foods, and live his last days smoking cigars and drinking strong cocktails. Haney enjoyed travelling more than ever. Once he reached India, he didn't think of the financial woes and health issues back home. He understood there was more to life than worrying about the consequences. He accepted the worst-case scenario, and once he stopped obsessing over his problems, they disappeared. After his time travelling the world, Haney sold back his casket and kept living his life.[1]

Litchfield's and Haney's stories lead us to question our own worries. When was the last time you made a decision only to second-guess it? It's a familiar pattern we as humans go through. We constantly question if we did the right thing and whether or not there's time to change our route. It's often the case we forget to analyse the facts of the situation, leading us to extended periods of unwarranted stress. If you lose a job, you can get another one. If you require surgery, you can bounce back. If you get a divorce, you've gained significant life experience.

We often perceive our current state of worry as the be-all, end-all. But in reality, our current state is an opportunity to manage our ego and gain strength in humility and experience. The mind is incredibly powerful and can make even the healthiest of humans feel ill.

If you pay close attention to what you're thinking and how you feel, embracing the worst-case scenario can often help calm you down. You're pushed into a forward-thinking direction where you can start to learn and live more usefully. You can't directly influence how you feel, but you can control your feelings through your thoughts and actions.

The simple way to feel happier for any human being is to be kind, not engage in bitterness and simply perform the act of happiness. Think of what you currently have and what you're grateful for.

The next time you experience worry and uncertainty, allow

yourself to *feel the feelings* and accept the facts. Assume and embrace the worst-case scenario and start working to improve it. When we stop worrying and start living, life becomes increasingly more valuable. We look to improve and do great things, gaining wisdom and a sense of purpose along the way.

When I first started writing, I would produce work but never publish it because of a perceived lack of interest. In my mind, I was fearful of whether or not it would be received well by my audience (or lack of audience). The more I wrote, the more work I would put aside, wondering if I'd ever return to it. Interestingly enough, as Pillar One comes to a close, a lot of the words you've just read were written years ago but hadn't seen the light of day until now. I rewrote much of this book several times, but still kept the majority of my ideas. Essentially, worrying was a replacement for the work I had been doing. My worry was a counterproductive way to ensure nothing got done. The truth is, we've all experienced this at some point. Think of it this way:

- A musician creates hundreds of songs, but only fifteen might make it on the album.
- An employee holds back from being themselves at work out of fear of being shunned.
- A person may not admit their fondness for someone out of fear of being rejected.
- An entrepreneur might not launch their product because they fear it won't sell.

The most common cause of our worries exists in the work we do and the relationships we have. For instance, high-pressure jobs tend to produce more anxiety and illness than a tranquil job. At the same time, marital problems and financial woes place a cloud of confusion over the future. The problem of being caught up in distress and worry presents itself in how we internally analyse the situation—because there's so much confusion, we continually overthink and struggle to deal with our anguish.

Tommy Caldwell embraced his fears and emotions when he

climbed the Dawn Wall. JK Rowling focused on the act of writing to control her life spiralling out of control. Galen Litchfield faced his worries head on and Earl. P Haney simply didn't let opinions and facts stop him from living life.

It wasn't mentioned in the beginning, but the rebel Tommy Caldwell pushed off the cliff in Kyrgyzstan was found alive after Tommy's return to the United States. It serves as a reminder for us all: the emotions you have are *always* the first to react in the face of perceived reality. If Tommy escaped knowing the rebel was still alive, would his emotional experience alter? Would he have done anything differently in response? What about Beth's experience? I don't have the answers nor the reasons.

But to answer the original question of Pillar One: why do we do anything at all?

We do things because we care about creating an ideal life. Your previous experiences and actions have defined the habits you have—some good, some bad. They have defined how you respond and continue to respond. Pillar One provided insight into understanding your current responses and actions. The pillars to come serve a more practical purpose in creating and living a rewarding life.

While it's important to understand why we behave a certain way and how we act, it's just as essential to recognise that simple actions produce consistent results. A lot of our internal battles come from overthinking and mind confusion. We occasionally try to think *too deep* in search of clarity and understanding, and we get caught up in the negative aspects of our lives. It can be a catch-22 because if we do the opposite, we might end up ignoring our problems and repeating the same damaging behaviours. Where do we draw the line?

Your experiences, the emotions you have, the lifestyle you live and what you consume are unique to your life alone. But there's one answer I can give you: For us to apply ourselves and live uniquely purposeful and effective lives, we're required to continue working on our ego and our emotions and be wary of how we live and whether it's in line with the direction we want to go. From here on in, I provide you with knowledge and confidence to cast out and reel in what you're good at and what you love so you can perform the tiny actions required to live a life worth living. Because, if there's anything you can take away from this book, let it be your ability to break through limiting beliefs and gain the tools required to act and perform in an optimal way.

7

UNDERSTAND YOURSELF: SUMMARY

- Focus on the value of what you do and who you do it for.
- Choose to *do something* remarkable.
- Applying consistent effort and humility in the areas you value keeps your ego quiet and your confidence high.
- When you practise the act of courage, fear becomes secondary.
- The solutions to your negative behaviours often lie in other areas of your life still waiting to be uncovered. Spend time on what's working first.

PILLAR II

THE CHOICES YOU MAKE

"A podium and a prison are each a place, one high and the other low, but in either place your freedom of choice can be maintained if you so wish". – Epictetus

Not one day goes by where you don't make a decision. You decide what time to go to bed. You decide whether you show up for work each day. You decide on what hobbies you learn. And while many of those decisions are automatic and based on your current routine and lifestyle, we're guaranteed to face choices that alter what we're used to—for the better or worse. Pillar Two: The Choices You Make provides insight into the mechanics of your decision-making and how you can influence and respond to choices that arise when faced with expected and unexpected challenges.

It's a timely transition because as we become more understanding of what's important to us and our direction, we begin to consciously connect the decisions we make. To put ourselves in the frame of mind between what's important to us and our decisions, we can look at a truly remarkable story of what happens when you stand by your values and make decisions in the face of consequences.

A perfect season. The dream of every athlete. No injuries, no losses, just the ability to win and keep winning.

In 1951, the United States was a country plagued by segregation and prejudice. Despite the 1776 signing of the US Declaration of Independence where it was written "all men are created equal," African Americans were still considered second-class citizens hundreds of years later. But the San Francisco Dons were years ahead of the nation, fielding its first integrated American football team in 1930. The 1951 University of San Francisco football fielding white and black athletes was rare but reflected the values of the university and city. The team was one of the most dominant college football teams in its era, with nine players going on to play in the NFL and three of those players eventually inducted into the Hall of Fame. Under the guidance of head coach Joseph Kuharich, the Dons went on an unbeaten 9-0 perfect record to finish the season. The team was so dominant that toward the end of every game, fans would pull out their handkerchiefs and sing Lead Belly's classic song "Goodnight Irene" to the opposition.

Following their 20-2 final game win over Loyola of Los Angeles, the team train rolled into Third and Townsend Street Station, packed full of USF players. When the team arrived back to San Francisco, they were set to receive their prize for finishing the 1951 season with an unbeaten record: an invite to the Bowl games—North America's most prestigious college football games, where the best teams compete at sold-out stadiums around the country. The Bowl games are highly sought after by every college football team in the country.

One by one, as the players emptied out of the train, they were met by head coach Kuharich. Coach Kuharich had news for the team, but it wasn't the news the players expected. Of the three major Bowls in the south—The Gator, Sugar and Orange Bowl—only the Orange Bowl had extended the invite for the Dons to play. Here stood a team with a perfect season record only extended one invite. To their further dismay, the Orange Bowl's invite came with certain conditions: the Don's were told that if they were going to compete, they had to leave behind African American stars Ollie Matson and Burl Toler. The players were dumbfounded. They stared at Kuharich as he stood quietly, understanding the team's gut-wrenching pain. The team gathered together for a few minutes and spoke amongst themselves. After some discussion, the Dons decided to meet with the Orange Bowl committee. The meeting was tense, but the committee wouldn't back down. After a few emotional words, white American backup quarterback Bill Henneberry yelled, "Go to hell! If Ollie and Burl can't go, none of us go!" The entire team walked out of the meeting, and that was the end of it.

The San Francisco team made it clear that the relationship with two of their most talented players meant more than playing in a legacy-defining game. It so happened that the USF's decision was kept under wraps by the Orange Bowl, and Georgia Tech was selected to play Baylor. Their motive was to make it look like USF was never chosen.

The most astonishing aspect of the Dons' decision wasn't that they passed on the Orange Bowl, but that the team never realised the magnitude of their actions. Their decision to side together as a team came before Rosa Parks and Martin Luther King Jr. It came well before civil rights leaders were standing up to the conditions that plagued the world. USF were already losing $70,000 per year on their football program and by participating in the Orange Bowl, the team would have covered their debt. In their decision to stand by their values, they turned down payment that would've fulfilled the football program's needs.

To this day, remaining players still talk about that decision during their annual lunches. Before the football team announced they wouldn't attend the Orange Bowl, Coach Kuharich had already resigned and moved on to coach NFL's Chicago Cardinals. The team's senior players had already started thinking about looking for jobs or fighting in the Korean War. The players who still had eligibility, more notably the younger players, either stayed in school to honour their scholarships or transferred to a different university.

In 2008, during one of the '51 Dons annual luncheons, one of the remaining team members, Dick Colombini, noticed a different crowd. Midway through the lunch, a spokesman got up from his seat and announced he was from the Fiesta Bowl. The Fiesta Bowl was created in 1971, a few decades after the USF Dons instrumental season. The man spoke on how unjust it was for the Orange Bowl to treat the African American players and team the way they did. He wanted to try making amends, announcing they would invite all living 1951 Dons to join them in a halftime tribute during the next Fiesta Bowl, held in Arizona. The players took the opportunity and were flown to Phoenix. They were treated with respect, staying in nice hotels, eating at nice restaurants and being wined and dined. After the treatment in Phoenix, Colombini started thinking, "What's next?"

Not long after, NFL Films approached the group about a movie and ESPN called them with their idea. Their idea came off the back of the attention that author Kristine Setting Clark set in motion. Clark wrote the book *Undefeated, Untied and Uninvited*, where she pushed George W. Bush and Barack Obama's administrations to bring the team out to the Whitehouse for a visit. Clark wanted the country and world to know how extraordinary the '51 Dons were because of the decision they made to forgo the Orange Bowl and the repercussions of that choice. Their decision wasn't just about making a statement. It was about doing the right thing. It was about fighting for their friends, supporting family and instilling values within themselves and their community to stick together.

The documentary *'51 Dons* aired during Black History Month in 2014 by ESPN Films. From the '51 football team, the two African American stars achieved remarkable feats in their own right. Burl Toler became the first Black NFL official in 1965, and Ollie Matson won a bronze medal in the 400-metre sprint and silver in the 4x400-metre relay at the 1952 Olympics in Helsinki.

During those days, the initial choice to put African American players on the field in itself was extraordinary. That choice reflected the values of San Francisco, the Dons and the players at a time when African Americans remained second-class citizens. Giving up a national college game that would bring the USF football program out of debt and giving up an opportunity for other players to experience a famous game set significant precedence. It was an unselfish act, but it was also a stand against racism. It was an act of social justice. It was emotional intelligence at its highest and a decision ultimately bigger than themselves. In the face of consequence, the '51 Dons were the real winners. At the core, the remarkable story of the 1951 Dons teaches us that the big decisions we make should align with what is truly important to us.

Succeed or fail, win or lose. It doesn't matter if your results are personal or professional. The decisions you make are dependent on the quality of your thoughts. When you produce ideas, you're banking future decisions that can influence your behaviour. Thinking allows us to make sense, interpret and mould our experience to make the best prediction possible. The thoughts we engage with brings our attention to the overarching point of Pillar Two: Your actions depend on the choices you pursue. The quality of your life and destiny are directly connected.

Each day you make decisions that reflect your priorities. You decide to eat breakfast in the morning. You choose what outfit to wear. You decide whether you'll go to the gym. But we face more challenging decisions as well: Which career should I pursue? Should I take a pay cut? Should I start a new business? Should I stay or leave my relationship?

When deeply thinking about hard decisions, we tend to forget about the easier decisions we make throughout the day, leading to a loss in routine combined with clouded judgement. We must acknowledge how and why we arrive at our choices in order to make optimal decisions. The how comes from your current, daily actions, and the why comes from the results of those actions. What behaviours are you currently making that influence your positive or negative choices? For instance, do you decide to stay at work late even though you're aware this choice increases your stress? On the contrary, do you choose to make time to enjoy learning a new skill simply because of the increased enjoyment you gain?

Choice reflection brings in a fundamental question: should you focus on your small, daily choices or should you heavily invest your mental resources to large-scale decisions? Using the previous example, if you want to manage your stress and stop working so late, practise making smaller but effective decisions that reduce the friction of overtime labour. Whether that's saying no to unimportant meetings or not responding to unnecessary emails, these small decisions allow you to consistently leave work on time.

Decide to say yes to what's important, then take consistent action on the small-scale choices. The following chapters of Pillar Two explore how we make decisions, an essential component of saying yes to a rewarding life. In this section, you'll establish your process of decision-making so you can focus on making small, daily choices that encourage your direction.

8

DECISION MECHANICS AND THE PROCESS OF DECIDING

Right or wrong, big or small, fast or slow. When making decisions, we aim to balance the outcome of our choices with the risks involved. Our decisions can be instantly satisfying, or chosen on the premise of long-term pleasure. Decision-making has been studied in many domains: statistics, sociology, economics, psychology, political science and more. Much research has been dedicated to the mechanics of how we arrive at the outcomes we seek. Understanding your own decision-making begins with aligning your current thought process with an area of focus. Arriving at effective decisions can be achieved by understanding the two different thought systems we engage with: System 1 and System 2.

When we mentally process how we will proceed, the speed at which we choose is either fast or slow. Popularised by psychologist Daniel Kahneman in his book *Thinking, Fast and Slow*, System 1 is defined as the rapid, unconscious choices we make driven by personal experience and emotion. System 2 is defined as the slower, more analytical and deliberate process of making a choice. While both systems compete for the same outcome, System 1 wins out when under pressure while System 2 is strained. System 2 earns its victories in deliberation, rationalisation and self-control.

Figure 8.1 identifies the differences in their simplest form.

System 1 (Fast)	System 2 (Slow)
The answer to 4+4 is...?	The answer to 456 x 95 is...?
Driving on a quiet street	Reverse parallel parking on a busy road
Detect happiness in a voice	Monitoring your behaviour in social situations
Being in the comfort zone	Being in the learning zone
Complete the phrase "better late than..."	Complete a market research survey

Figure 8.1

When thinking deeper on the decisions you make, you identify more with System 2. We believe we are conscious, rational individuals who make decisions based on our beliefs, values and goals. For example, when applying for a job, we rationalise which choice to pursue based on the potential money we would earn, whether or not the job aligns with our career path and if the position would be enjoyable. We design our world based on the choices we make. Those choices then form the basis of habitual, patterned living. You might see your patterns as valuable—for example, going to the gym at the same time each day or spending every weekend with your family. In contrast, there could be patterns you'd like to change. For instance, working long hours, not exercising or consuming too much social media.

Although System 1 is critical to consistency and seeing results in how we live, we fall short of our potential if we spend the majority of our time in System 1. We tend to think and respond quickly, failing to slow down and survey the landscape in order to choose where we could direct our energy and focus. There's often a familiarity in how we live. We know which desk to sit at when we get to the office. We turn on the TV when we arrive home. We drive on autopilot, using the same route to work every day. It's only when we encounter something out of the norm that we engage System 2. And for us to improve an area of focus, we're required to spend more time and exertion rationalising and thinking.

There are, however, benefits which System 1 provides. It often submits feelings, impressions, intuitions and intentions to System 2. If System 2 endorses these suggestions, you're able to voluntarily apply actions with purpose. For example, if you regularly eat unhealthy food, System 1 can translate that guilt into your conscious mind. You're then faced with the decision to put down the unhealthy option, or continue as you were. But the problem arrives when we're not ready to make that decision or when our attention is directed inappropriately. To eat healthy and make an adjusted decision, System 2 should be activated by dedicating more mental resources to that system. You can achieve this by asking yourself certain questions which require you to think deeper in search of the reasons underneath your behaviour: Why do I continue to eat poorly? Am I emotionally eating?

That thought process is much tougher, but it can be remarkably rewarding when leveraging System 1 and engaging in the practices of System 2.

Maintaining this type of thinking proves challenging because you're required to do something that doesn't come naturally. You have to exert continuous effort, all while monitoring your own behaviour. To successfully transition conscious thoughts into unconscious actions, there needs to be a balance in resources towards each system. If you have too many options, you aren't performing optimally in your chosen area, meaning the choices you make are not in line with your direction. To overcome these difficulties, focus on the one thing you want to improve and practise asking yourself: *what is one decision I can make today that would make everything else easier?* Here are some examples:

- Not eating can prove challenging when making basic decisions throughout the day. But eating a full, nutritious breakfast makes it easier not to snack and primes your day for focus.
- Having a messy desk can bring a feeling of overwhelm. But cleaning your desk at the end of each day increases productivity when arriving at the office the following morning.
- Waking up and rushing to find your gym clothes can start your day on the wrong foot. But preparing your clothes the evening before means making one less decision when you wake up.

MENTAL HEURISTICS

To make optimal decisions in the benefit of your goals and desires, we should be aware of the mental heuristics which influence our choices. Heuristics, in this instance, are the mental shortcuts your brain takes to arrive at a decision. For example, when you see a hooded figure in a dark alley, you might walk a bit faster or avoid walking down the alley altogether. Another common mental shortcut we might make is watching the news about an aeroplane crash and letting it affect our travel plans.

Heuristics work for you, but also against you. Let's look at the upside to mental heuristics: they help with problem solving, simply complex questions and help us arrive at a conclusion faster. The downside, however, is that heuristics increase your chances of making decisions that are not in your best interest. There are different heuristics to be aware of: availability heuristic, anchoring, confirmation bias, and survivorship bias. Let's go through each of these in more detail.

. . .

Availability Heuristics. Quite often, we make a decision based on the information which automatically comes to mind. Consider an executive who is required to promote someone to fill a managerial role. They've narrowed the decision down to two candidates, both possessing strong leadership skills. However, the two candidates have both made significant mistakes in the past. The first candidate forgot to submit their work on time, and the second candidate went on holiday without delegating their work. The executive remembers the first candidate's mistake more vividly because they weren't directly affected by the second candidate's mistake, even though the gravity and consequences of both mistakes were the same. The executive then promotes the second candidate. As another example, consider an investor who judges the quality of an investment based on what he's seen in the news. He ignores all other relevant facts or trends and acts solely on the information he's come across.

Because information is readily accessible to us, we tend to overvalue what we can remember and undervalue what we don't know.

Anchoring. When we make a decision, it's possible to rely heavily on the first piece of information we learn. The initial information can then be used as an anchor or focal point to make our choice. For example, studies have demonstrated that when a criminal judge has recommended a prison sentence by the lawyer of the defence, it has a significant effect on the judge's decision. When given an anchor (ie. a ten year sentence), the judge is more likely to prosecute a higher prison term.[1] Anchoring often occurs without thought. For instance, the national average price for petrol in 2003 in Australia was roughly 90c per litre.[2] People were used to paying that price, but over the years, the national cost crept up and consumers had to adjust their anchor. In 2020, the price of petrol increased to 142c per litre. Consumers considered this expensive, but if they got fuel for 120c, it would be a bargain. So at one point, people thought paying more than 90c was ridiculous, but years later they're happy to pay 120c.

We can use anchoring in our favour. Consider these examples:

- Negotiating a salary: When negotiating how much you'll earn to a potential employer, rather than communicate what you'll settle for, offer a higher figure. Your potential employer is likely to either accept, or offer a figure less than your original sum. Either way, you can be satisfied with the offer.
- Writing: When you struggle to put words on a page, double your goal for what you would normally produce. If your goal is to write 250 words, double it to 500. Raising the focal point produces satisfaction even if you don't reach the full 500.
- Saving money: Rather than transfer left over money into your savings account, set an anchor of when and how much you will transfer so it grows consistently over time.

Confirmation Bias. Perhaps the most common form of mental error. Confirmation bias bases itself on receiving previous information related to existing or previous beliefs and values. When we look for information that supports an existing belief, we have the tendency to unintentionally make biased decisions and reject new data that goes against what we believe in.

For example, in 1998 Andrew Wakefield's controversial study linked the measles vaccine to autism.[3] It was retracted from the British Medical Journal in 2010 after the presentation of evidence showing that Wakefield had manipulated the data. His confirmation bias powered his aspiration to establish a link between vaccinations and autism. The claim is disproven today but still remains a topic of discussion in the medical world. It's not natural for us to form an opinion and test it in different ways to prove it false. It's more likely we prove it true and use the information around us to support that conclusion. We prefer the information we seek to be validating rather than new. If we explore our thoughts impartially and are open to evidence which disproves our thoughts, our ability to limit confirmation bias proves valuable.

Survivorship Bias. When we study and consider the successful outcomes of others, it's likely we ignore the failures that came with their success. For example, in World War II, the American military asked mathematician Abraham Wald to investigate how to stop war planes from being shot down.[4] The military knew they could use armour as protection but couldn't protect the whole plane.

The initial plan was to examine all planes returning from combat. They would analyse where those planes had been hit the worst, and reinforce those areas. Although the returning planes were examined, the American military failed to investigate the aircrafts that didn't return. As a result, the military armoured up the wrong parts of the plane, focusing on the areas which *didn't* require protection. This type of mental error is survivorship bias.

We experience this in our lives consistently. For example:

- When a new song is released on the radio, we might say, "Music was so much better in the 90s". We're comparing the song to past decades and their success at that time.
- When reading success stories of our idols, we believe we can mirror their success by doing *exactly* what they did. Unfortunately, the information we consume doesn't present *all* the data necessary to emulate their success.

- We read reviews of products all the time, but don't consider those who *didn't* write a review. Product reviews often don't tell us the whole story.

Because all success factors aren't considered, we're prone to make ineffective decisions. When we forget who lost and only remember the winners, our decision-making strategies have the potential to become compromised.

The brain is remarkable at performing mental errors. We're prone to slipping into a pattern when using them in a situation which doesn't align with our direction. Rather than thinking of these errors as a fatigued mind or our inability to make correct decisions, consider them a verification that the shortcuts we take aren't always useful. Self-awareness and your ability to analyse your confidence is the key to making optimal decisions and setting yourself up to take action on what you seek. There are a few different ways we can do this: take time away from the noise, practise discovering all options available to you, and act from the place where your passion and values lie. Those are the most important decisions.

Take time away from the noise. Overwhelm and stress undoubtedly have the potential to cloud our decision-making, leading to ineffective choices. Demands from our personal and professional lives compete with our minds for attention. All too often we succumb to the pressures of daily life. In today's world, there's no shortage of reasons to feel anxious and overwhelmed. But there are solutions to the chaos life brings:

- Stay connected with others. Stress and anxiety can cause negative feelings which fosters isolation. Make the decision to ask for help from a trusted source and still maintain positive communication with those who provide it back.

- Plan ahead. Give yourself something to look forward to, whether that's catching up with a friend or making time for a skill you love learning. Create opportunities for what you enjoy.
- Live simply. Much of the reasons behind our chaotic world is represented in the overanalysing and mental battles we engage in. Bring yourself back to a simple world where any progress is still progress. Simple steps, simple living. Not everything has to be complicated. At the core of your clouded decision-making lies simplicity. To bring control back to your life, ask yourself, how will I feel tomorrow or a few days from now? More often than not, you will acknowledge that the anxiety and overwhelm will pass and you're able to control your decision-making more effectively.

Discover other options available to you. Optimal solutions are not possible without solid alternatives. We frequently choose a single solution without weighing what else is available to us. For example, a manager who hires someone outside their company based on skills and resume may forget to look internally. They potentially miss out on hiring the employee who has company knowledge, loyalty and the right attitude to perform the job exceptionally well. Identify what other options are available so you can be confident and aware in how you make your decisions.

Act in the interest of your passions and values. This is where becoming fully clear of what's important to you gets put into action. Your awareness of your passions and values allows you to navigate through challenging situations. With what you seek constantly in the back of your mind, you're skilfully able to make the optimal decisions required to get you back on track whenever you deviate from your chosen path.

THE PROCESS

Our decisions represent the challenges and uncertainties of life. How we respond determines our place in society. The success in the parts we play as a manager, husband, wife, father, writer, athlete, entrepreneur, student and every other role relies on the choices we make. Making good decisions is a fundamental life skill and something individuals universally strive for. Some of our decisions are obvious and require less deliberation with minimal consequences. But there are those which require a great deal of self-reflection and assessment. For example:

Should I go to university?
Am I willing to change careers?
Will I have children?
Where should I live?
Should I earn more money but remain unfulfilled?
Will I learn a new skill?
How should I invest my savings?

There's no easy or obvious solution to these questions and, more often than not, these decisions have an effect on those around us.

We dread making tough choices because they bring anxiety, fear, uncertainty and regret and expose us to the judgements of others. Our discomfort leads us to making quick, impulsive choices or, more commonly, not deciding at all. Sometimes we'll even let luck define our fate. The good news is, we can learn to respond to the tough questions we ask ourselves through a few conscious steps.

Step 1. Identify The Decision and Objectives

It's essential to identify *what* choice you're about to make. Ask yourself:

What am I trying to achieve when I say yes or no?
How will this decision benefit my life?
What do I want to be known for?

Think of your decisions as a form of goal-setting and self-reflection to gain a vantage point for all other decisions which come along the journey. If we can't identify the choice we make, we increase the risk of making ineffective decisions and going in the opposite direction we intended. For example, you may be faced with a decision to quit your job. Is it a new career you're chasing, or is it a different boss you're looking for? When you identify the objective of the decision, you avoid making an unbalanced choice.

Acknowledge your ultimate goal. Think of it like this: I start at A, but what do I want when I get to B? When you think through your objective, clarity starts to arrive, leading you towards the right path. "I started an exciting career, but have outgrown my potential and I now seek a role with a larger company".

Step 2. Choose Your Alternatives

Your alternatives represent the range of potential choices available when pursuing your objective. Because we're prone to dwelling in failure from one choice, we should acknowledge the different approaches that present themselves. For instance, imagine a person looking to lose weight, but all of their programs consist only of running. They lost a little bit of weight, but an injury puts an end to the routine. Instead of deciding to wait until their injury heals, the person focuses on other aspects of fitness, like lifting weights and keeping their metabolism in check.

When choosing alternatives, there are trade-offs to consider. To complete this book, I allocated a small amount of time per day over a lengthy period. I sacrificed attempting to complete it as quickly as possible because I had a full-time job and valued the time spent in my relationships and learning the skill of boxing. For me, it wasn't sustainable and effective to rush the process. When accepting alternatives in any decision, there are trade-offs to consider:

- How much time will I sacrifice to learn something new?
- Am I willing to earn less in the beginning to make more in the future?
- Am I willing to forego family/friend events in order to reach my objective?

Your alternatives are not a single action, but a set of actions that create an approach to reach your objective. I had to be willing to trade a quick turnaround time for a slow, monotonous process.

It's important you take enough time entertaining all factors available. When we don't engage in this method, we can overlook opportunities and courses of action which push us towards our objective. To find your best alternative, ask yourself:

Am I overlooking anything?
If I did XYZ, what would happen?
What could be possible if . . . ?

Remember, we can never choose an alternative we haven't considered. There might be an incredible house available to rent around the corner, but if you're unaware of it, you won't move there. No matter how many alternatives you have, your choice can be no better than the best of the lot. Thus, the payoff from seeking new alternatives can be extremely high and significantly rewarding.

Step 3. Follow Through and Measure Your Actions

Once you've self-reflected and allocated your decisions, then physical action is required. The most effective way to achieve this is to align a behaviour with an action towards the objective.

For example:

- Objective: Lose weight
- Action: Hire a personal trainer
- Objective: Start a new business
- Action: Book a call with a business coach

Whatever your objective, performing the first step provides confidence to take the next step. Clarity extends itself from the *"thinking stage"* to the *"doing stage"*.

Although implementing actions bridges the gap between our objective and success, without a way to measure how we're doing, we risk seeing ineffective results. Stay vigilant in what's working and not working. If one alternative isn't serving you, then it's time to choose another. Many of us waste precious time performing actions that aren't benefiting our objective. To clarify what you're measuring, ask yourself:

How will I know when progress is made towards my objective?
How can I specifically measure my progress?
When will I know I've achieved my objective?

Step 4. Remain Flexible

As we strive to reach our objectives, things don't always pan out the way we anticipate. We experience unexpected troughs among the expected peaks. Along the journey of taking action on your decisions, your path may likely change and you'll need to alter the course.

Let's look at some unexpected scenarios in the case of the previous two examples that would prompt a change of course:

- Objective: Lose weight
- Action: Hire a trainer
- **Unexpected situation: The trainer leaves and the gym shuts down**

You have no control of this situation, but you can control how you respond—and how quickly you respond. What alternatives have you found that would get you closer to where you want to go? Accept that a change of environment will produce positive results, whether that's a new trainer in another gym or a different coach in an outdoor setting.

You have control over your response to unexpected situations. Your objective should remain the same and you should always think of making smaller adjustments so you can continue to make optimal decisions towards your goals. Whether it's the case of choosing a new alternative or reflecting on where you want to be, trust in the decision-making process to create direction and clarity.

9

HAVING TOO MANY CHOICES

When was the last time you struggled to find a new TV show to watch? After watching something brilliant, we need the next show to be just as good, if not better. Nowadays, there's plenty of options to choose from, you'd think it would be easy. When searching for something new, we're spoilt for choice, where Netflix's algorithm is based on what shows or movies we like or any new releases. We spend fifteen minutes trying to decide as we listen to the painful sound our TV makes as we continue scrolling. More often than not, we revert back to something we've already seen because of our indecisiveness. The problem isn't the lack of options; it's having too many.

Unfortunately, the overabundance of choices isn't limited to Netflix. Every day we're forced to make hundreds of decisions. Some of those are automatic, and others require a little more mental capacity.

While each decision we make may seem inconsequential, they have a cumulative effect on our performance throughout the day. When we make continual decisions, we're prone to decision fatigue, leading to poorer choices.

Social psychologist Roy F. Baumeister defines decision fatigue as the deterioration in our ability to make good choices after a process of constant decision-making. Essentially, the more decisions we're required to make, the worse our educated decision-making will be, resulting in low self-control and minimal willpower.

Judges are prone to decision fatigue. Researchers from the National Academy of Sciences examined the factors that impact the judgement at a criminal's parole hearing. The psychologists examined 1,102 judicial rulings over a ten-month period.[1] The rulings were based on whether or not the criminal would be released from prison on parole. It's easy to assume the decisions made by the judges would fit the crime and not depend on what time of day the prisoner has their hearing. But researchers found the complete opposite:

Case 1: The parole hearing took place at 8:50 a.m. and involved an Israeli serving a 30-month jail sentence for fraud.
Case 2: The parole hearing took place at 3:10 p.m. and involved an Israeli serving a 16-month jail sentence for assault.
Case 3: The parole hearing took place at 4:25 p.m. and involved an Israeli serving a 30-month jail sentence for fraud.

Of these three cases, only the first prisoner was granted parole. Even though cases 1 and 3 had similar sentences, the third prisoner did not receive a favourable hearing. The results confirmed that, from the 1,102 cases, judges ruled favourably 65% of the time. For prisoners appearing later in the day, they were granted parole only 10% of the time and those judgements were less likely to be deemed fair. The results indicate that the judge's decision didn't come from bias—they came from decision fatigue.

In a similar example, Dr. Jean Twenge conducted an experiment based around the impact of decision fatigue in relation to self-control.[2] In the first part of the experiment, Twenge assigned each group to either decide between a product or rate their consumption. The groups were as follows:

Choice Condition Group: Participants were given a list of sixty products (pens, pencils, scented candles, magazines etc.) They were asked to read from the list provided and choose between two versions of the product (e.g., a blue pen or a red pen, scented candle or unscented, etc.).

Non-Choice Condition Group: Participants were given the same list, but were instructed to rate the products from their most used to least used.

Results showed that the choice condition group used far more mental resources in the experiment. The participants who made choices among the products were more self-involved in the task than those from the non-choice condition group. Upon completion, the participants moved immediately into the second experiment. This task aimed to test the hypothesis that making continual decisions depletes our willpower.

In what Twenge called the cold pressor task, both groups had been asked to submit their non-dominant arm into near-freezing water for as long as possible. The idea of the task was to see how the groups overrode their natural tendency to recoil and pull their arm out. Twenge predicted that the choice condition group wouldn't be able to overcome the impulse more than the non-choice condition group. Her prediction proved true.

Those who made a series of decisions previously were the ones who removed their arm from the water the earliest. Based on the two tasks, participants who experienced decision fatigue from the initial experiment lacked the willpower to keep their hand in the water for as long as the non-choice condition group.

This leads us to a universal assumption: Each decision we make adds one more dent to our willpower.

The more dents you have, the harder it becomes to focus, resulting in minimal energy and impaired decision-making. Similar to the mental errors we make, the consequences of decision-making show up in different ways:

· · ·

Decision Avoidance. When making too many decisions, we begin to neglect or ignore the other choices available to us. This type of behaviour results in choosing the option most socially acceptable instead of choosing the option most beneficial to us. For instance, procrastination is inevitably a form of decision avoidance. We delay our decision for another day or until the need to decide disappears altogether. When we experience this, we ultimately work against what we want to achieve. This avoidance results in fewer opportunities to align our behaviours with our direction, placing high, and unnecessary, stress on ourselves.

Ambiguity Effect. People have the tendency to avoid choices which bring uncertainty. And because those decisions require more intensive and complex thought, when they're ignored, we make poor choices. The ambiguity effect can be considered a mental heuristic, much like confirmation bias and anchoring. To understand the ambiguity effect in action, imagine searching for a new washing machine online. You're looking at two options and they both do the exact same thing. To make a more informed decision, you begin to look at the reviews of each washing machine. One has an average review rating, while the other product has no ratings since it's just been released yesterday. Even though the washing machine with no rating could potentially be better, we feel more comfortable knowing what we're purchasing. We play it safe by buying the average rated washing machine and risk missing out on the potentially better product. When making decisions like these, we aren't giving equal weight to the possibility that taking a risk could benefit us.

Impulsive Decisions. When making quick choices with little thought, we tend to regret the outcome. Impulsiveness occurs when our willpower's gas tank is empty and our thoughts become exhausted. We experience this in the grocery store all the time. When chocolate bars are placed next to the checkout, it influences our decision to purchase one. Because we've already made many decisions on what to put in our basket, when we reach the checkout, we purchase the chocolate bar without much thought.

Beyond the grocery store, there are other areas which influence our impulsive decisions. For instance, if we're really hungry, we're likely to make a quick choice on what food to consume. If we're stressed, we're using our willpower to control our behaviour and lose the ability to be reflective. If we had a long day at work, we might forgo the gym for an evening on the couch. In our heart, we want to exercise, but our brain is exhausted and looks for a way out.

Decision fatigue works the same no matter whether you're exercising, learning a new skill, showing up to your job, or working on your side business. It's something we all deal with and will continue to deal with. The good news is that you can apply strategies to keep your willpower tank at least half full, if not completely full. Even with half a tank, you can continue being smart in the choices you make.

Strategy #1: Remove yourself from life's mayhem. Some of your best ideas originate in tranquil moments. When you place yourself in a quiet environment, you're pulling away from daily demands and using the part of your brain that doesn't allow you to exhaustively think and consume. The brain has a proclivity to present us with knowledge that we weren't previously able to tap into. When stepping away from the urgent demand's life throws your way, you improve neural connections, ultimately leading to better decision-making. It's why meditation, exercise and socialising are known antidotes to a clouded mind. To step away from the chaos life brings, take a breath. Pause for a moment and allow yourself to separate the space of what's urgent from the intention in your decision-making.

• • •

Strategy #2: Limit your decision-making when hungry. Most of us don't think about *how* we make choices when on the search for food. When we have an appetite, our body produces a hunger hormone known as ghrelin—facilitating the sensations of hunger and fullness. Our levels of ghrelin fluctuate during the day, depending on food intake and metabolism. When ghrelin isn't regulated, it negatively impacts our impulse control and decision-making. Consider this the next time you're making important choices. Ask yourself, am I aligning my food intake to support my daily decisions? This allows for a state of focus when weighing our options. A fool proof, practical way to manage your appetite is to eat small, frequent meals and keep your protein intake strong so you're satisfied more often and your mind stays sharp.

Strategy #3: Establish a ritual. The difference between a ritual and a routine lies in the attitude behind the action. Routines are considered something you *have* to do, like making the bed, brushing your teeth, etc. A ritual, however, is a more meaningful practice and provides a sense of purpose. By establishing a ritual, we can limit the number of decisions we make each day.

For example, one of my rituals is writing each morning Monday to Friday. It's a meaningful behaviour that results in significant production over time. When I write each morning, I'm more inclined to perform better throughout the day. For you, you might go out for a coffee or go for a swim. A purposeful ritual is designed to conserve energy and make optimal decisions throughout the day. Think of what daily or weekly actions you can perform that create purpose. Then begin to implement those actions as often as you can.

Strategy #4: Live simply. Whether you seek to improve performance or control consumption of any kind, the biggest frustration in this process is using every ounce of willpower every day. Instead of fighting against it, find a way to simplify your life. The insignificant decisions we make syphon precious energy and willpower from what's important. To live more simply, audit your days and see where you can make one decision which would normally require many decisions for the same outcome. Here are some examples:

- If you make one decision on what to eat each evening for dinner, you save more willpower. Preparing your food ahead of time reduces the number of future decisions that week.
- Making a decision each day about whether to exercise can be insignificant, but having a scheduled program increases performance and reduces decisions like what exercise to do at the gym that day.
- If you're an online business owner, keeping up with marketing demands can be challenging. But spending a few hours to schedule your social media posts for the week allows you to focus your energy elsewhere and improve performance in other areas.

What's remarkable about our ability to make decisions is being able to bundle our daily choices into one overall decision, which frees up our time and, more importantly, our energy. Scattered, quick and often mentally consuming decisions can turn into planning, preparation and significantly reduced dents in our willpower. If you stay ahead of the game, you can make sound decisions on what's important, setting yourself up to implement the right behaviours.

We make a lot of low impact choices, so it's essential to review the decisions we make every so often. For example, if you want to spend more time practising a hobby or skill, you can look at your current choices which hold you back from achieving this. If you find yourself becoming too distracted in other areas, pinpoint the repetitive decisions that cause that distraction.

Self-diagnosis of your small, daily choices helps you take

action and become aware of the changes required so you have clarity on working towards the bigger decision at play. In the instance of practising a hobby or learning a new skill, the change from distraction to action can be as simple as having a conscious plan for what you would like to achieve that day, or as effortless as knowing what you'll do when you wake up in the morning. When you begin to become aware of your automatic actions, you identify your level of willpower. It then becomes easier to avoid making repetitive and impulsive decisions that don't serve your priorities.

10

BE THE ARCHITECT

On the 11th March 2011, the most powerful earthquake ever recorded in Japan shook the country's eastern coast. A quake so vicious, it shifted the earth from its axis, triggering a tsunami that swept over Honshu—the main island of Japan. It reached a magnitude of 9.0 and killed eighteen thousand people, wiping entire towns off the map. Trouble also hit the Fukushima Daiichi Nuclear Power Plant when an enormous wave hit the building and flooded reactors, sparking an immediate threat to lives. Authorities set up an exclusion zone as radiation began leaking from the plant. One hundred and fifty thousand people were forced to evacuate, and over a decade later, most residents have never returned home.

Following the tragedy, a study evaluated Japan's transparency in communicating information, advice and opinions (known as risk communication), and the influence those communications had post-disaster on individuals and the Japanese public as a whole.[1] The method systemised the effects and validity of risk communication based on nudge theory, a human behaviour technique designed to influence decisions and behaviours. The study was based on how risk was communicated to individuals, and measured through media coverage, personal radiation levels and thyroid examinations (extreme radiation exposure can cause thyroid cancer). The study discovered the following results.

The impact risk communication had on individuals: After the Fukushima disaster, an individual could either be told that "there is 0.1% cancer risk from the radiation", or instead be informed that "even though there is 0.1% chance of cancer risk, there is a 99.9% chance it won't affect you". This suggests people are "nudged" according to how the information is presented, even though both sentences carry the same information.

One year after the disaster, Japanese media shared results from a white blood count survey, revealing that internal contamination from radiation wasn't detected in more than 94% of the participants.[2] The media could choose to share whether 6% were internally contaminated or show whether it wasn't detected in the 94%.

In the public environment: In Minamisoma, children were expected to get assessed for radiation levels, while for adults, getting assessed was communicated as "those who wish, could be tested". This approach reflected the parents' expectations of radiation education. In 2013, 98% of children were tested, while only 15% of adults showed up for testing in the same year.

In the city of Date, the local government began distributing personal dosimeters for children and pregnant women in regions with high radiation. Less than a year after the disaster, they were distributed to every resident. People could refuse to accept a personal dosimeter, but using one was considered the norm. Those residents who used the digital dosimeters were nudged to think about radiation and ended up with heightened anxiety than they previously experienced.

· · ·

The nuclear disaster is an example of how we can become encouraged to make decisions, especially decisions which heighten our mental stress and anxiety. The Fukushima evaluation brings up questions we can ask in our own lives: How do we determine what a good decision is? And who is determining whether something is good for us? Assessing the answers to these questions helps us eliminate negative influences that push us towards poor decisions. When you evaluate the decisions available to you from the perspective of nudge theory, you can optimise choices more effectively—not by expecting a "better decision", but by being aware of how you're being nudged into a negative action loop.

When we're looking for a shift in behaviour, we can apply the psychology behind nudge theory to various situations. For instance, at Schiphol Airport in Amsterdam, authorities used a small, fly-shaped sticker in urinals so men had something to aim for. It influenced their subconscious behaviour, and spillages in the bathrooms reduced by 80%. The tactic has now been applied in urinals throughout the world. When applying a nudge, you're more likely to make a direct choice that aligns the behaviours favouring the desired outcome.

We aren't entirely rational, so the nudger uses techniques to alter one's environment, affecting our subconscious decision-making. We may have experienced these methods in the following ways:

- Fast food chains ask if you would like to upgrade your meal, a tactic used to increase revenue. But the opposite has also worked. A study found that some Chinese restaurants had waiters ask customers if they would like to downsize their meal, and 33% of the patrons downsized, reducing their intake by approximately 200 calories.[3]
- When hotels reduced the plate size in their restaurants, they were able to reduce food waste by

22%. Patron satisfaction remained the same, and they barely noticed the smaller plates.
- The train station in Stockholm, Sweden, made the stairs look like piano keys. The idea nudged those who normally took the escalators to give the stairs a go. Traffic on the stairs increased 66% and the idea has since been applied in other big cities.

While these are just a couple of examples, there are different types of nudges to become aware of:

Setting a default option. It's common to stick with the one option presented as a default—we're more likely to choose it. For instance, we often select the standard shipping method when online shopping but ignore the next day delivery method. The Fukushima study shows a default option in action—children, they said, should be assessed for radiation levels, but adults had a choice. Getting tested was the default, not getting tested was the option.

Using a psychological anchor. We rely on an initial piece of information to decide. For example, when deciding on which online subscription to purchase, there is often a recommended package that influences the choice we make.

The ease of available options. This involves making a good option easier or a bad option harder. If you want to eat healthier, you could get rid of the chocolate in the fridge. When you start to have cravings, the decision to drive down to the shop is a much harder action than opening the fridge.

• • •

Different nudges can be used in various situations and applied to other cognitive systems. When thinking of our decisions in systems, our automatic and fast (System 1), and conscious and calculated (System 2) thoughts come into play when applying choice architecture. A fast-food worker would provide the default option of "would you like coke for the drink?" targeting our System 1 (automatic) response system. Conversely, when dealing with a real estate agent, they would inform us of the benefits of purchasing a particular property. This particular nudge targets our System 2 (slow) response system, requiring more conscious thought to make an informed decision.

Nudges work because we solicit irrational thinking when making decisions. To apply the appropriate decisions, you're required to internally assess your current environment and figure out two things:

1. What currently helps me make the right decisions?
2. What keeps me from making beneficial decisions in line with my goal?

One of the main goals individuals and organisations have is to improve overall productivity, happiness and well-being. Applying our own nudges in our lives can enhance an effective decision-making environment.

Every day you choose what to eat and drink, if you'll exercise and what social media platform to open up. And because you're not always up for making decisions that benefit you, we're required to understand how certain strategies can eliminate negative choices to encourage making the right ones.

The solution begins with analysing different areas of your life. What decisions do you consistently make that you'd like to avoid? Consider your answers in line with the below:

- **Health.** Do I want to improve my physical and mental health?

- **Finances.** Am I looking to buy a house? Am I happy to keep renting and saving or do I enjoy being more relaxed about my funds?
- **Relationships/Friendships.** Am I seeking a partner? Do I need to reach out more to my current friends and put in more effort?
- **Career.** Am I satisfied with my current career path? Is there a part of me that wants more from what I'm currently doing or do I want a change?
- **Hobbies/Skills.** What do I enjoy? Is making money from a hobby or skill something that interests me? Will I make time to practise?

When you're transparent in where you direct your attention, ambition helps you make the right decisions based on the goals you set. There are different nudging tools which encourage better choices:

Using reminders and prompts. You might set your alarm in the morning on your phone and name the alarm based on the action you will take. It might say "Wake up to read". This prompts you to apply the necessary action when waking up.

Decide on different framing. You can frame your decision as either one step closer or one step farther away. If you go to the gym, you're one workout closer to achieving your goal, but if you miss a day, you have one more day to catch up. Framing defines the positive and negative trade offs in the actions you take.

Manipulate the accessibility. If eating healthier foods is one of your goals, you're more likely to make the healthier choice if you remove all unhealthy foods from the pantry and fridge. Similarly, if you have the tendency to be distracted by your phone, disable notifications when working on important tasks.

Social pressure and self-commitments for accountability. If you're socially active, communicating your progress to your friends and family encourages decisions that support your goals. You receive motivation to keep moving forward and accountability that pushes your actions to become part of your identity.

There are various thoughts and needs pulling us in different directions, competing for attention in our body and mind. Self-nudging not only helps us resolve internal pain points, it also promotes self-understanding of where you can improve and align your decisions correctly. When encouraging yourself to make more beneficial decisions, it's far more effective and sustainable to change something by 1% instead of 100%. Practise altering one or two areas in your life and focus on the smaller decisions required to improve your behaviour. The more you practise, the more awareness you'll have to overcome the more significant challenges ahead. When creating a successful nudge, ensure it a) decreases the efforts required so you're using less willpower, and b) improves your motivation to act on a choice.

Use these tactics and strategic self-reflective questions to your advantage so your decisions are in line with what you set out to achieve.

11

WHEN OVERTHINKING OCCURS

It can be the cruellest of situations. There's no moment in football like stepping up to take a penalty kick during a shootout, where the spotlight shines on one player to kick the winning goal. If the player scores, there's a celebration. But miss a penalty, and the hopes of an entire team, and often an entire nation, fade.

The most heart-breaking penalty miss in history came from Italy and Brazil's 1994 World Cup Final. Roberto Baggio is considered one of Italy's greatest strikers in history. He scored five goals in the 1994 campaign, leading Italy to face South American powerhouse Brazil in the World Cup Final. The game would finish in a draw, forcing a winner by a penalty shootout for the first time in the tournament's history. When Baggio stepped up to the spot, he needed to score to keep his team in the game. If he missed, Brazil would become World Cup champions. Baggio took a deep breath. He approached the spot and kicked through the ball, opting for power over precision. The football sailed high over the crossbar, leaving Italian supporters in anguish and the team in despair. As Brazil celebrated, Baggio could only wonder how he missed a routine target in such a stunning fashion.

. . .

Studies on what causes individuals to miss penalty kicks have overbearingly shown that the kickers' anxiety and the mental pressure they find themselves in can adversely affect performance.[1] Researchers asked ten experienced football players and twelve inexperienced players to participate in a penalty-kicking task. There were three rounds with specific conditions:

Round 1: No goalkeeper was present and labelled as a practise round.
Round 2: Had a goalkeeper who was friendly and wasn't allowed to put the kicker off.
Round 3: Had a competitive and distracting goalkeeper, with each kicker competing for a prize.

Participants had five rounds each and wore functional NIRS headsets which measured oxygen changes to the brain. All participants performed well in the first round, but significantly poorer in the second and third. The inexperienced players performed worse than the experienced players, an outcome which can be based on the assumption that they were less skilful and less able to deal with the mental conditions the goalkeeper presented. The most significant findings were that the penalty kickers missed more shots when they showed more use of the prefrontal cortex, an area of the brain used for long-term thinking.

This manifests itself as what's known as choking under pressure. Furthermore, the study suggests that poor performance at the penalty spot comes from overthinking and contemplating the consequences of failure right before the action is performed. In Baggio's situation, many thoughts could have transpired throughout the game which led to missing the penalty. Thoughts built up until the final moment, when he had to decide how to approach the kick.

For many of us, overthinking occurs in different areas of our lives: our relationships, the career we pursue, the goals we set, the skills we learn, etc. It's a common characteristic because we want to ensure we cover all available information. Overthinking doesn't just cause us to make irrational decisions, it also has the potential to stop us from making any decision at all. Overthinking occurs when:

- We are overwhelmed by our options.
- The process is overcomplicated.
- We are fearful of the consequences.
- The decision needs to be perfect.

We attempt to use these causes to control a situation and feel more confident with where we're at and where we're heading. But all overthinking does is prevent us from taking action because we can't shift our focus from overanalysing.

Like most obstacles, practise becomes the aim when overcoming issues. There are two main areas of concern that affect your ability to overthink: the fear of failure and perfectionism.

The Fear of Failure. Failure regularly induces fear. When you fear a lack of success, you allow yourself to stop taking action on what's important. The key is to expect failure. When failure arrives, leverage your mistakes by evaluating the outcomes in the decisions you made. For example, if you're starting a business and haven't sold any products, what's the reason behind it? Do you have a marketing strategy in place? How are you measuring sales? We can't achieve what we don't see, but when we see results more significantly through failure, we can be more clinical in approaching a different decision with the same outcome.

Additionally, you can reframe how you set your goals. When you overthink, you're already mentally defeating yourself. Failure should include both learning and growing. Get into the habit of asking yourself, what will I learn from this? You might have a goal of earning ten thousand dollars from a new product launch. Although specific, include what you could learn from the product launch. The ten thousand dollar target remains, but you also decide to anchor a learning experience. Failure then doesn't seem too bad if you don't reach the target because you've learned something of value.

Never underestimate the power of wisdom through failure. Knowledge turns into clarity and sets you up to overcome the fear in making decisions. We allow fear to dictate our decision-making because we don't like feeling it. But if you open up to feel the fear when it shows, you'll notice it begins to disperse and encourage a more coherent response. The next time you find yourself fearing failure and thinking more than you should, ask yourself: What can I learn from this situation? How can I grow from this experience? What are two or three positives to take away? You're then able to fail forward and, more importantly, fail into confidence and success.

No matter the outcome, you grow throughout the process and become more resilient and confident in bouncing back from failure. Leverage your mistakes and make realistic assessments by reminding yourself there's still so much to learn and achieve. Your failures are a direct link in the chain of achievement.

Perfectionism. Perfectionism is a spectrum of tendencies that lead you to think, "If what I do isn't perfect, then it's terrible". The focus of perfection is limited, with eyes only on the destination instead of the journey. The common assumption with these characteristics is that the relentless pursuit and need to be perfect produces highly effective work.

Attempting to get our decisions correct 100% of the time is well entrenched in our ability to overthink. Sometimes our standards are too high, and we're unable to tolerate making mistakes, assuming the consequences are worse than they are. A perfectionist overthinks because they live by being, and choosing perfectly. The outcome of this type of thinking leads to replaying and criticising their mistakes and feeling inadequate. The approach to goal-setting tends to be inflexible, with an all or nothing mindset. Although perfectionists are extremely motivated and highly engaged, the relentless pursuit of success can produce little reward.

Professor Brian Swider analysed and compared ninety-five studies surrounding the topic of perfectionism and found no evidence that perfectionists perform better, nor do their higher standards lead to higher-quality work.[2] When perfectionists achieve exceptional results, that's what they come to expect, and they find it hard to celebrate their wins. The unrelenting pressure to achieve their desired success results in a lack of satisfaction and can fuel unnecessary anxiety and stress, leading to burnout. Perfectionism arrives in different forms. Some are mild, others are more severe:

- Spending half an hour overanalysing a draft email before sending it
- Comparing ourselves to others and comparing unfavourably
- Difficulty in being happy for others

Although the examples share similar behaviours, there are three sources where perfectionism extends itself.

1. Self-Oriented Perfectionism. Those who practise this type of perfectionism adhere to high standards which motivate them in their life and career. Self-oriented perfectionists are associated with greater productivity and assertiveness in decision-making. Their goals also energise them without becoming overwhelming or paralysing.

2. Socially Prescribed Perfectionism. The self-critical individual who feels relentless pressure to perform at their best and who also has a fear of rejection. There's perceived external standards which contribute to socially prescribed perfectionists' destructive decisions (social media, family, workplace, etc.).

3. Other-Oriented Perfectionism. Perfectionists who are other-oriented hold others to a higher standard and are critical to judgement. It can be hard to collaborate on projects and networks due to this person's judgemental decisions.

Can you relate? Although we can be healthy in our approach to perfecting what we seek, it's often overshadowed by detrimental decisions stemming from overthinking our results and failures. To overcome this way of thinking, we're required to give up our desire to believe our journey will be smooth sailing. Taking action is a messy process from start to finish. Although decisions can sometimes be simple, our thoughts and emotions can lead us to expect more from the outcome.

To control and reduce perfectionism, practise being comfortable with your negative emotions. Allow yourself to experience being second in the pursuit of success. When was the last time you saw a leader admit to their mistakes? What about the last time you saw someone post their failures on social media for the world to see? Just like our fear of failure, we need to be okay with not winning them all. Remind yourself that taking action and completing something is *always* better than perfect. As I've continually reminded myself when writing this book: done is better than perfect.

LIMIT OVERTHINKING

Being bombarded with options creates an environment that challenges us to the point of being paralysed to make decisions and consistently overstep our approach. Awareness is the beginning of decision change. Many of us obsess about the future, forgetting to be present and live through each moment.

Before you begin to address how you think, you must address your surrounding thoughts. Are you consistently letting others dictate your decisions? How do you respond when faced with challenges? Identifying with moments of awareness plants the seed to begin prioritising suitable choices. From there, you can differentiate between the decisions that require immediate action and those that can be attended to later. A commitment to clarity provides a route for clear thinking, leading to an effective outcome from the decision you make.

Most of the decisions we make are not life altering. If your perfectionism causes you to behave detrimentally, choosing a "good enough" decision might be your best option. Good enough decisions keep you moving forward, limiting the opportunity to paralyse yourself by not deciding anything at all.

However, not all decisions should be made on our own. There are times when seeking advice from a trusted source becomes the more valuable option. Seeking trusted opinions provides new angles to a choice we didn't see ourselves. Is there a trusting friend you can seek out to talk with about a personal problem? Does your coach offer sound advice in upgrading your skills?

We need to use our judgement to determine if the advice given to us is in our best interest. Whether or not we listen to others and their opinions depends on our relationship with the trusted source and our previous experiences with them.

Have enough faith in yourself to shift your inner dialogue from "not good enough" to "more than enough". If the inner critic takes the lead on self-talk and overthinking, you won't be clear in your decisions. Regulating your thoughts and acknowledging the sources which affect your choices provide the gateway to a positive mindset, where decision-making becomes the strength and failing forward becomes the lesson.

12

LEARN TO PLAY THE LONG GAME

In the late 1960s, researcher Walter Mischel conducted an experiment, methodically tormenting children using marshmallows. More than five hundred parents volunteered their kids to participate in the examination; a famous study known as The Marshmallow Test. The purpose of the research was to understand a child's ability to wait in order to obtain something they wanted. The process began when researchers brought a toddler into a private room. The room had zero distractions, and on the table, the child had two options to choose from: a marshmallow or a pretzel. There was a method to the madness. If a child ate their first treat within fifteen minutes, there wouldn't be a second. One treat now, or two treats later. Some children quit as soon as Mischel read the testing conditions. The researchers studied the children's behaviour as they sat for fifteen minutes, engaging in different kinds of delay tactics. Some would close their eyes and hover over the treat, while others would stare into the abyss, hoping they would outlast the researchers. On average, the children held out for less than three minutes, and only three out of ten managed to last until the end. It became apparent to the researchers that most children weren't able to employ self-control, thus short-circuiting their willpower.

The Marshmallow Test wasn't made famous because of the

nature of the "torture". The revelation came years later, where Mischel found out that how these children behaved in the study corresponded with the decisions they made as adults. Mishel undertook two studies decades later of the same children where he discovered unexpected correlations between the results of the original marshmallow experiment and the success children had as they got older.

In 1988, the first follow-up study showed that the children who delayed gratification longer in the original marshmallow test were described by their parents more than ten years later as competent teenagers. The second follow-up study in 1990 showed that those who delayed gratification also had higher school test results in comparison to those who ate the original treat.[1]

These results are, of course, limited because of the unknowns of the child's home environment, cognitive ability and background. But as adults, these studies beg the question: Why is it so hard to stay the course on our long-term goals when we know that sticking to them far outweighs the benefit of putting them off?

The instant gratification cycle is real. We're consistently tempted to forego a future benefit to obtain a less rewarding but timely comfort.

We face our own marshmallow test nearly every minute of every day.

As a culture, we live in a world where it's expected to have anything right away with minimal effort. When we surrender our long-term goals for short-term activities, we seek real-time rewards. We indulge in immediate pleasures, ultimately resulting in long-term pain. We only have to look as far as technology to see the cause. Every day we're mindlessly tempted to open browser tabs, scroll aimlessly through our phone, do some online shopping, look at Instagram and Facebook and consume all the constant pieces of information that do to us what marshmallows do to toddlers.

Our impulsive nature enables reasons and excuses not to

perform our desired actions because of the suffering it creates at that moment, even though we know our desired actions will ultimately benefit us. Humans tend to go to great lengths to avoid momentary pain, especially during times of vulnerability and weakness. We self-sabotage ourselves to feel good immediately, indulging in temptations at a high cost. Unfortunately, this doesn't work in the long run. We must give to get something back. Your ability to delay rewards is vital because the actions you take determine the trajectory of your life and success. Overnight success is a myth because when we see someone rise to the top quickly, that's all we know, leading us to attempt replicating their results. But we don't see that person's full narrative of patience, failure, hard work and small achievements. It's why playing the long game is more fulfilling throughout the journey because we're working towards something remarkable. If you want to succeed in an area of importance, then at some point in time, you need to find the discipline to promote action instead of engaging in what comes easy.

There are everyday decisions to weigh in our lives which determine whether we're held back or moving forward:

- We go to the gym and eat well for a week, but the weight hasn't come off and we haven't gotten any stronger. We give up and hope that something else will work.
- Putting money in the bank to save for a house is the aim, but online shopping and unnecessary spending becomes the game. The cycle repeats, and we are no better off than six months ago.
- We want to wake up early and start the day. Instead, we hit snooze and sleep in. It's been three months, and we're still tired all the time and haven't attended the early gym session we promised to ourselves.
- When starting a new business, we're on a limited budget, but we buy a new laptop, rent office space, and spend more than we should hiring assistants.

These examples come back to the question: *what is important to you?*

Without a reason to delay your rewards, there's a significant struggle to reach the heights you expect from yourself. Ensure you have clearly defined goals pointed towards what you want to achieve long term. They should be effective enough to convince you to make the right decision and put in extra work. The next pillar unlocks how to set the *right* goals with the *right* intentions.

Understanding your objectives and what's important to you puts you on your bike and in a position to execute a plan. As you ride along for the journey, you're reminded of the daily choices you need to make. For instance, imagine someone looking to start a business. The person values their vision and understands their objective, so they come up with a plan to hire a coach. They begin consuming knowledge, engrossing themselves in a community and taking action to grow the business. Because they have guidance, clarity and support, it's much easier to say no to the decisions that don't support their goals. We should all find support. Delayed gratification doesn't work well without the help of others.

When it comes to achieving what we expect, receiving future rewards can take weeks, months and even years to arrive. This is why you're required to be kind to yourself. Without an enthusiasm to take action, your decision-making skills become compromised. Although time is considered our greatest commodity and we want to get from A to B as quickly as possible, it's how we show up each day that affects our results. When you reach a milestone along the way, simple strategies like buying something you've had your eye on or enjoying a night without feeling guilty lets you know you're appreciating life without being a victim to your sacrifices.

The more you practise making the right decisions based on long-term outcomes, the easier it becomes to progress. You have an unconscious mind that's responsible for unnecessary thoughts, feelings and memories. Unlike young children, adults are characterised by their ability to delay rewards and tolerate hard work, discipline and vulnerability to fulfil their responsibilities and achieve their goals. Delaying gratification brings a whole range of benefits by promoting your well-being and objectives. Again, ask yourself, *is what I'm doing today really helping me tomorrow?*

You must be able to want what you force without forcing what you want. Auditing what you consume and where you spend your time creates the conviction to play the long game and invest in your actions instead of unnecessarily spending them elsewhere.

13

DECIDE TO MAKE AN IMPACT

Ryan White was an American teenager who grew up in Kokomo, Indiana. Doctors diagnosed him with haemophilia type A at three days old—a hereditary blood coagulation disorder caused by an unfortunate circumcision complication at birth. At age thirteen, Ryan became highly ill, battling pneumonia. The doctors ordered a lung biopsy, and when the results came back, Ryan tested positive for AIDS. He had received contaminated blood treatment in a blood transfusion required for haemophilia therapy.

After his diagnosis, it wasn't until a year later, Ryan started feeling stronger and was keen on returning to his classmates. His mother asked if he could attend school, but officials rejected the request. There had been significant pressure within the Kokomo community. One hundred and seventeen parents and fifty teachers signed a petition to keep Ryan out of school. The ignorance regarding AIDS was transparent throughout the United States, causing reason for fear. Ryan's family put through a formal request to the public school district, but it was declined by the superintendent. They decided to take the matter to court, eventually winning the case, allowing him to return. But after his first day back, Ryan was taunted and shunned by other students. Vandals threw rocks at the windows of the White family's house, and shop attendants refused to touch hands when accepting change from his mother.

The experience was harrowing, and in 1987, the family relocated to Cicero, Indiana, a new area almost an hour away. Ryan was enrolled at Hamilton Heights High School. The principal welcomed him with a firm handshake and encouraged the student body to engage in informative discussions on HIV/AIDS. One of those students was Jill Stewart.[1] She brought in medical experts to talk to the children and began educating their parents on the history and cause of the disease. The children went home and educated their parents. This was a time when homophobia was truly entrenched, and people had unfounded fears of how the virus was transmitted, leading to systemic prejudice towards young, sick children. It was clear Ryan's battle was much larger than his disease.

The revolt against him denied Ryan's ability to spend time with his friends, get an education and live a relatively normal life like most children his age. Fortunately, his new school allowed him to make a difference in the lives of others. Ryan began to act on his disease, and his case became the national antidote for awareness. Ryan served as a persuasive AIDS spokesperson in his school, leading to further engagements with journalists, media and eventually the American public.

The thirteen-year-old fought against bigots that continually hurled abuse, believing AIDS to be brought upon homosexuals and who had done God wrong. During his pursuit of awareness, Ryan recommended that the national blood supply require immediate attention so that every donation could be tested for evidence of HIV. His impact started to build momentum. Between 1985 and 1987, the number of news stories on AIDS doubled. Ryan frequently appeared on national television and newspapers to talk about his tribulations and life with the disease. His fundraising efforts had celebrities like Elton John, Michael Jackson, Ronald Reagan and Nancy Reagan appear alongside him to destigmatise how those with AIDS could mix with the rest of society. Sadly, in early 1990, Ryan's health deteriorated. He hosted an after-Oscars party with former President Ronald Reagan in his final public appearance. On March 29, 1990, Ryan was admitted into the hospital with a respiratory tract infection. As his condition worsened, he was sedated and placed on a ventilator. Elton John was one of his last visitors before Ryan passed away on April 8, 1990.

A few months after Ryan's passing, President George H.W. Bush signed a bill known today as the Ryan White CARE Act. The legislation initially provided two billion dollars to help cities, states and community-based organisations develop systems and maintain the care and treatment of HIV/AIDS, specifically for Americans who were suffering the worst. The bill was due to expire in 2009 before Barack Obama agreed to an extension, where it still maintains its place in society today.[2]

As the poster child during the AIDS epidemic, Ryan's legacy lived on. His sheer motivation and circumstance led him to bring awareness to others as he set out to change a damaging environment. The confidence he personified at such a young age to speak on television programs, campaign for funds and educate in the face of prejudice and ignorance was truly remarkable.

But that's just it. *He chose to do something remarkable.* He changed an entire perception around the world with his actions.

It's a distinct reminder: What you choose to do with your circumstances is entirely up to you. You can make a difference in a chaotic, saturated world, and you can decide to take control of your actions. There's value in creating something of value, not for only ourselves—but for others as well.

THERE IS NO RIGHT TIME

There's a significant difference between your decisions and the action taken. Look around the room and acknowledge that everything you see started from an idea. The couch you're sitting on. The painting on your wall. The watch on your wrist. All initiated from a thought. Those ideas were acted on either by an individual or by a collective. Nothing is learned or experienced without action. Action gives us the belief that what we think we can also succeed in. To reiterate the point: A baby doesn't learn to walk by thinking about it. They spend hours of practice standing up before finally taking a step. The same can be said for learning to drive. We have to get ourselves into the car and put our foot on the accelerator to succeed.

One of the most challenging problems we face as adults is finding reasons we can't do something. It's easy to simplify and assume laziness is an intrinsic human characteristic. But there's more to it. Several conscious and subconscious reasons cause our inaction to become the reaction. For example:

1. Our comparisons in talent predict we're not good enough to impact ourselves and others. There's often tension between having the ability to do something and working hard to reach success. The most effective intervention for the fear of having little talent is to go against our nature and replace our toxic habits with those that lead us to action.

2. Instead of our brain functioning as the owner of thoughts, it assigns itself as a public relations manager. We're too worried about what others think and what they're doing, and we start to think that our inaction isn't socially acceptable.

3. We've done no self-reflection on what's important to us. We think about the results and outcomes of what we are trying to achieve but don't understand the process and journey required to get there.

4. Although dedicated in other areas, we aren't willing to give up to get back, which stems from our proclivity to be comfortable. Our time hasn't been reassessed, and we are still at the stage of worry.

Your ability to implement breakthrough measures depends on how you anticipate the outcome of your objective. Think of the action you take like a muscle. When you begin to lift weights, you attempt to perfect the correct technique with little weight. As you progress, muscle memory appears, and your strength improves over time. It's the same when you decide to act. The more you exercise action, the better you are at it and the stronger we become in cyphering out what's essential. We have a tendency to wait for the right opportunity and the right time to make or follow through on a decision. Often, we are waiting for motivation to arrive, other times we self-sabotage, putting ourselves in a worse position before seeking progress. The critical mindset to adopt when disrupting our improvements is to think of motivation as the outcome of progress. Recognise motivation as the last step, not the first. To bring clarity to your actions, ask yourself:

- What is the primary objective I'm searching for?
- How do I want to feel when I see progress?
- How does it improve my life, and does it improve others around me?

There's no perfect time, only the present time. If you wait for everything to be perfect before taking action, there will never be progress. Life continually moves forward and obstacles continue to present themselves. Taking action now allows you to make adjustments while you continue on the path of achievement. There's an ancient Chinese proverb which says, "The best time to plant a tree was twenty years ago, and the second-best time is now".

If you planted seeds twenty years ago, there would be an entire tree with shade today. But if you don't plant seeds today, twenty years in the future, you'll still be standing in the sun. Action is an investment into the future of who we want to be.

When writing this book, I often overthought the words I wrote. I'd think, is this good enough? Should I increase my word count? During those phases, I overanalysed to the point of getting nothing done. I had to stop obsessing and move forward. When I found myself paralysing my own work, I reminded myself not every day would be a good writing day. But action is, nonetheless, progress in itself. The outcome of this book involved many struggling days and many productive, forward-thinking days. The difference between what it was and how it is means not losing sight of performing the act itself.

There will be moments of anxiety during the process of living a rewarding life. But those moments help us muster up responses to jump through the hoops and practise the act of courage. Taking control of your life involves risk, and when you accept risk, you open up a range of diverse opportunities to thrive and succeed with. But without risk, you struggle to break free from your current identity, and the transformation you seek becomes a constant uphill battle to overcome.

The power of unequivocal progress comes from acting on what's important and being open to new solutions for improvement. You must be willing to experiment with new routines as you begin to advance through defining moments and milestones of achievement. Routines are important because, as you live through this world, your identity becomes created through the decisions you make and the habits you enact. Without taking action, those closest to us won't know who we are or who we are becoming.

The positive impact you create on yourself and others brings a sense and feeling of freedom that wouldn't exist without action. You have the capability to change how and where you spend your time without having it dictated by others. You can change careers if you're fed up. You can learn a new skill and be great at it. You can start a new business. All that's required of you is to decide and act on what is truly important to you.

Everything that is hard in life is made from a series of more manageable actions. You're not supposed to have *all* the answers right away, but remember: action creates traction.

In the next pillar, I focus on how you can make an impact on yourself and others by connecting your ideas and identity to the right goals. When you live with direction, your life becomes much more enjoyable. You may have ideas of your own that you want to act on, but feel it would take away from life's responsibilities, such as being a parent, a spouse or having a full-time job. The thought of having extra time to commit to your goals may seem near impossible, but the idea you have in your mind has the capability to break the limitations of time and the conditions you're in. You just need the right approach.

14

THE CHOICES YOU MAKE: SUMMARY

- Each decision you make reflects your priorities. To put your current decision-making in a better position, consider whether those priorities align with what you seek.
- When you bundle your daily choices into an overall decision, your energy frees up. Choose planning and preparation over scattered and spontaneous decisions.
- It's more effective to change 1% of your decisions rather than 100% overnight. Practise the smallest but most effective choices first. Once you nail those, practise making optimal choices in other areas. You will find those other areas become easier because the most effective decisions you've implemented early on continue with less resistance.
- Ask yourself, is what I'm doing today really helping me tomorrow? Auditing what you consume helps create conviction to invest in your actions and future success.
- There is no right time to decide. Nothing is learned or experienced without action. Decide now to start believing.

PILLAR III

ACHIEVING WHAT YOU SEEK

"Progress is not achieved by luck or accident, but by working on yourself daily". – Epictetus

There's an old quote: what you seek, is seeking you. It illuminates the idea that your thoughts and intentions draw good or bad things your way. But what can also be interpreted from this quote is the reminder for us to create the ideal reality behind our passions, purpose and values. Pillar Three: Achieving What You Seek transforms the decisions you make into purposeful and practical goals. Throughout the following chapters, you are clearing the road and paving direction while simultaneously creating space to perform specific, life-improving actions.

I'm reminded of an old friend, Louise, who once worked hospitality at the local pub my friends and I frequented. "Your friendly local" was the pub's motto, and she was always one of the friendliest there. She always had time for a drink and a chat after a long shift. At the time, Louise also worked at an engineering firm while balancing her job at the bar.

She eventually left the hospitality industry in pursuit of a corporate career and spent the following two years in a project assistant role. The job took a heavy toll. There were expectations that came with 6 a.m. office meetings and arranging breakfasts for managers, only to stay late after hours and finish proposals. Meanwhile, her direct boss worked from home, leaving Louise to cope with ever-increasing workplace pressure.

As frustrations grew, so did her need for change. She moved to a new role in project management in hopes that the new environment would provide a pathway to a fulfilling career. Louise found out very quickly she'd made a mistake, again becoming part of a corporate culture where it was assumed you'd miss lunch, work late and understand projects without the appropriate training. And on top of the pressure, Louise experienced workplace bullying that had become all too common in corporate industries. The only aspect she enjoyed was the social events.

But as it turned out, socialising with colleagues was another trap for ineffective office chat and unnecessary gossip—a recipe for sucking the time and life out of impact and progress. Right before the pandemic, Louise was made redundant. It was a pivotal moment where she realised how unstable her life was. She was left feeling incredibly small in a big world.

For Louise, she had two options: continue living an unrewarding life and go back to an unfulfilling job, or be bold, brave, and find a way to take action on her future. It was time for a change. Louise started to think deeply about the direction she wanted to take. She asked herself: What skills do I have? What am I good at? *What's important to me?* Helping people was at the forefront of her mind.

At thirty-one years of age, there was no time like the present to do something remarkable. She researched the charging rate of her current skillset and was blown away that she could earn two hundred dollars per hour. It was the lightbulb moment that catapulted her thoughts into action. She decided the skills and experience she possessed were too valuable to neglect. Rather than earn less and feel like a number in a company without any internal rewards, she could earn more, make a genuine impact on individuals and become filled with life again.

Louise got clear on the services she could offer that added value to small businesses. She conducted market research and hired mindset and business coaches. She set up a website, organised products, structured pricing, targeted ads through Facebook and Instagram and told anyone who'd listen about her new venture.

Louise put her skills and personality out there to the world and immediately found her audience. It took eight weeks to match her income from her previous job. Her belief improved as evidence began to stack up that what she was doing was working. Having inner faith made it easier to apply continual acts of courage, becoming a full-time virtual assistant coach and mentor for others. For Louise, her old lifestyle was behind her. She no longer had to sit in peak hour traffic, dreading the moment of arriving at her desk each day. Her clients are part of a community—a space where bullying doesn't exist and individuals genuinely support each other without judgement.

Her goals came to fruition through consistency and showing up each day. She visualised her long-term goals, backed herself and got back up whenever she got knocked down.

Today, Louise has built a virtual assistant community and gained financial freedom, waking up with purpose each day and creating *valuable* time in her day.

She lives a rewarding life as defined by her.

At the beginning of Pillar One, I asked you: *what do you want to be known for?*

You can act on a business idea.

You can advance in the career you love.

You can learn a new skill and become an expert.

You can write the book you've been thinking about.

• • •

When working on your goals, you won't always know how you'll get there or if you'll even make it at all. Pillar Three: Achieving What You Seek works through these obstacles so you can create a pathway that links who you want to become with the right approach.

It's easy to set goals, and it's easy to visualise what you seek. The hard part is sustaining the right behaviours and mindset to turn your thoughts into results. The path to achievement becomes much clearer if you have the right attitude and the right system.

15

CREATING A PATHWAY

We all introspect on what we aim to achieve: lose some extra weight, build a successful business, raise a family, write a book, retire early and the list goes on. But how do we get there? To be useful in setting the right goals, you need to evaluate the system that surrounds you. Too often the actions we apply aren't focusing enough on progress. We're too concerned with getting to the end as quickly as possible.

One of the biggest reasons for turning our backs on our goals is because we don't have enough structure to encourage the right actions.

Imagine setting up a new train line. You have a train, but need to create the tracks to secure its movement. After building the tracks, you create different stops along the train line for when you're on board. Think of your goals in this sense: Your goals become the train which provides you direction. The tracks become your system, guiding you from A to B. Each stop you land at becomes a progression point. If you arrive on a different track, you end up in a place you didn't intend to go.

Without an effective system, there's no direction and progress is limited. To navigate your way through your goals, you need to be clear in your process and understand *how* you will get there.

· · ·

The most effective way to align your systems and goals is to connect them to your environment. We often make choices based on the environment we are in, positively and negatively. For instance, you might exercise at a local gym around the corner from where you live. You then decide to move, which puts you an hour away from the gym. The challenge to exercise then becomes more difficult because it's a longer drive. Because you value your time, the likelihood of going to the gym becomes less than if the gym was still around the corner. What you end up doing instead is using that time to watch TV or something that doesn't benefit your goals. The more accessible the alternative, the more you're inclined to choose those. The alternatives are often negative because we have too many dents in our willpower to act towards a goal that suddenly becomes harder.

The choices you make in life are moulded by the options available to you. Too often we make it harder on ourselves to make progress when there's an easier choice staring us in the face.

Making progress on your goals requires an evaluation and calculation of where you currently sit. It's only when there's evidence of progress that you're more inclined to keep pushing forward. The human mind loves progression. When there's positive feedback from where you started to where you're heading, feel-good chemicals release into the brain, creating momentum and a pathway to keep believing and striving forward. Here are simple examples of how I've measured my progression in the past:

- When I measured the number of rounds on the boxing bag, my fitness increased.
- When I measured how many words I was writing per day, I wrote more.
- When I recorded how many pages I read per day, I learned more.

Measuring your goals works for breaking negative patterns as well:

- When I measured the amount of junk food I was consuming, I ate less.
- When I recorded how much time I spent on social media, I consumed less.
- When I measured how little time I spent with my friends and family, I spent more.

Through tracking and measuring, you get an idea if you are getting better or worse. Recording your progress is not about results, it's about understanding and discovering—to make sure your train is on the right track and heading to the right destination, consciously adjusting to what's working and not working.

BUILDING MOMENTUM

We often think the reason we give up on our goals is because we aren't seeing desired results. But our reasons go beyond that. We don't see results because we lack focus on who we would like to become. When you're struggling for motivation and momentum, ask yourself, what do I want to be known for? You might be motivated to lose 10kg. While you have a specific goal, you need to consider an identity along with it.

You need to *become* the type of person that goes to fitness classes or walks every day. To truly build and apply momentum, recognise it as a three-step process: clarify the goal, review the process and change your identity.

Step 1: Clarify the Goal. Do you want to publish a book? Lose weight? Get a promotion? Consider the goal as surface level thoughts to your results. They're what's waiting for you at the end of the line. To reach the outcome, you need to go deeper and build the tracks required to begin moving forward.

Step 2: Review the Process. Your processes are the habits and systems you implement to reach your desired outcome. Your process could be writing 500 words a day, showing up to a fitness class three times a week, or identifying and solving new workplace problems. What small habits can you apply that encourage results? The majority of the habits you build are connected by reviewing your current process.

Step 3: Change Your Identity. Adjust the judgements of yourself and others. When your identity is clear, you build momentum more effectively. Don't be someone who writes. *Become a writer.* You're not someone looking for a promotion. *You're a leader.* You're not someone who goes to the gym every day. *You're an athlete.* Decide on the type of person you want to become and prove it to yourself by taking small, simple steps which focus on the process rather than the outcome. Learn *how* to improve.

It's all well and good to have a process, but there's a fine line between progression and consuming material to help get us there. When trying to gain motivation and inspiration, we have the tendency to watch YouTube videos, read the perfect article or seek success stories. Although this type of inspiration can be motivating, it's limited in its ability to maintain momentum. The pathway to achievement becomes blurry when we become too much of a consumer and less of a creator. It makes it hard to build and maintain momentum when we're stuck in a constant loop of seeking information.

To keep your mind clear for action, limit the amount of what you consume by engaging in only one or two important sources of information as opposed to seeking many answers from different areas. Limiting your sources opens up more room, energy and time to focus on what's practical and build identity-based habits so that you become someone you're proud of—an individual who achieves the outcome you envision.

A SIMPLE STRATEGY

To achieve any goal, implementing smaller, more manageable milestones along the way is key. The small wins we have represent the progress points along the journey. They keep you on track.

- If your identity is to become a writer and the outcome is to publish a book, a small win is to write 250 words each day.
- If your identity is to be a great friend and the outcome is to be well respected by those close to you, a small win is to call a friend every weekend.
- If your identity is to become a leader at work and the outcome is to be promoted, a small win comes from getting to the office earlier and planning your day/week.
- If your identity is to become an athlete, a small win comes from showing up to the gym when you're tired.

When you do the little things well, they compound over time. Each time you arrive at a small milestone, your ability to maintain your trajectory through progress substantially improves because each small achievement feeds into your existing behaviours and you begin to feel and see positive shifts in your progress.

It's important to not rely on motivation. Your system should be set up in a way which manages your motivation and is beneficial to your outcome.

The most effective strategy is to focus on breaking your goals down into smaller steps. For example, if you want to get promoted, there's different steps you can implement to get there:

Step 1: Ask your manager for new challenges.
Step 2: Stay focused on challenging work.
Step 3: Get proactive and set your own performance review.
Step 4: Ask for feedback.

Each step provides an opportunity to build on what's next. If you ask for new challenges, you're more likely to give it your all when they come your way. If you set your own performance review with your manager, you're more likely to ask for feedback.

The momentum you generate makes it more desirable to keep going. The small victories create a ripple effect, providing an ever-increasing dose of intrinsic motivation, taking you one step closer to your desired identity and desired outcome.

Small wins > Momentum > Generated Movement = Results.

When we run into setbacks, it's tempting to throw in the towel and give up. By learning to modify your approach, you can find new routes that still keep you on track. Rather than change your goals, changing your strategy is often the first point of call. For example:

Outcome: Run a marathon
Current Strategy: Run 15km once a week
Setback: Only reaching 12km at your best when the marathon is a month away
New Strategy: Run the marathon two months after your original date to give you more time

Outcome: Become a high-level manager
Current Strategy: Working in a current role for a promotion
Setback: Made redundant
New Strategy: Apply current skills in an alternative industry or stick with the same industry and seek out job security

Outcome: Lose 20kg
Current Strategy: Run 4x per week
Setback: Hitting a weight loss plateau
New Strategy: Implement weight training to increase metabolism

When modifying a setback towards your goals, start with one small change. Too many changes have the potential to throw your system into chaos. If one modification isn't working after a few weeks, try something different and see how it goes. The changes you make from a setback aren't a sign of failure. They're an essential part of staying the course and keeping your momentum going.

Finding intrinsic motivation, though, can be a challenge. This is why choosing who you would like to be known for is important. When you know your chosen identity, you gain extraordinary meaning and clarity in your behaviours and align them with your goals. Having an identity provides the structure to build your system towards the outcome you're chasing. When you break down the desired result into small wins, momentum will be hard to stop.

WHEN SHOULD YOU CHANGE YOUR STRATEGY?

We frequently change our strategy as we get older because the goalposts are continually moving. As teenagers, we go to school and learn. As we get older, we attend university, work full time, have a family, get married and come across all those life-altering moments. The goalposts shift throughout our life stages, as does our approach to living. While your life strategies continue to change, you should fixate on adapting your approach to what's important. In your current environment, which areas are you excelling in, and which need improving?

Here are some examples of changing strategies in different areas of your life:

The Foods You Consume. What foods do you currently eat? When do you eat them? How much do you eat? These questions determine your strategy into eating more/less or adding/removing foods that help you perform better. If you're an office worker looking to lose weight, audit how much food you consume during the week. There are free apps that make it easy to track your consumption and base your strategy on whether you're eating too much or not enough. Adding/removing certain foods/drinks from your diet can be the difference in reaching your desired health goal.

Exercise. A sprinter would incorporate strength and explosiveness into their training. A marathon runner would incorporate long-distance running and endurance into their regime. If a sprinter had a marathon runner's strategy, they wouldn't reach optimal performance. Determine your exercise goals to implement a plan. Do you want to lose weight? Increase your strength? How much time do you have per week to exercise? Your answers to these questions will determine the strategy you take, whether that's hiring a personal trainer, exercising more/less or training differently.

Professional Career. You may want to take on more responsibility at work and get a promotion. Ask yourself, is it about the money or the career? You might be content with what you're currently doing and want to maintain your performance. What can you focus on that helps drive you in the direction you want to go? Additionally, we should always remember that a career provides a focal point on something for the rest of your life. The hobbies and passions you have allow you to become someone outside of everyone's expectations. Ask yourself, if I could do something free for the rest of my life, what would it be? Work towards building a career out of your answer by gathering information about your interests. That's what Louise did.

Productivity. After reaching the end of the day, there may be tasks you wish you had done. You wish you had completed a report, made it to the gym or had dinner on time. Thinking about the important behaviours that require action every day based on your goals helps you understand what you're doing that's unproductive and determines the strategy to work on the essential things.

When we don't perform well under our current strategy, it creates unnecessary stress and can crush our spirit to the point we give up. For example, you may want to wake up at 6 a.m. every morning, but you sleep in for another hour. The first time you sleep in, you become annoyed with yourself. The second time, you're still annoyed and tell yourself you'll try again tomorrow. You then sleep in for three days in a row, and it becomes an ingrained thought that waking up at 6 a.m. will be something you will always struggle with.

You're not sleeping in because you're not a morning person. Your strategy needs to change. You might need to go to bed half an hour earlier or not eat right before bed. Try different ways to help you wake up better, bearing in mind that practise and persistence is a prerequisite.

When setting a business strategy, entrepreneurs make choices around certain factors. Is the product at a low or high price? What's the quality of the product like? What location will the product be supplied in? The questions and answers determine the type of strategies applied for the business to perform. We can use this concept to determine our approach to our own lives. For example, the failures we encounter often cause us to change our goals when we should ultimately be changing our strategy:

- A business idea which fails often doesn't lack the vision or the passion. It lacks the right strategy.
- An employer whose team consistently is underperforming isn't because they're hopeless. They're underperforming because they need training and direction.
- A writer who fails to publish their work doesn't fail because they're a terrible writer. They failed because they had no confidence in their writing.
- An athlete who consistently struggles with performance isn't required to change sports. They just need to practise their weaknesses.

While it's fair to change our strategy when we aren't seeing progress, it's equally important to refrain from changing our approach when progress works in our favour. Don't fix something that's not broken. If your goal is to continue losing weight, do more of what's working. If your business revenue continues to increase, keep the same strategy. Continue on the working path, focus on what you can control, and create continual progress that aligns with your outcome.

16

YOUR MOTIVATIONS

Centuries ago, humans were driven to search for food, water, and a safe place to sleep. Those basic needs drove humanity forward. But when economies began manufacturing goods, the motivation factors for humans changed. The world became more complex—the search for food and water no longer guided us. In today's environment, humans rely on extrinsic motivation to produce goods and services, where the type of motivation stems from external rewards and punishment. The strategy behind this type of motivation implies that rewards reinforce desirable behaviour and consequences prevent the undesirable.

We can see how this effect impacts modern-day office workers. If an employee earns a high salary in a corporate role, they'll likely respond more effectively in their position. Conversely, if an employee is given a written warning because they continually run late, that consequence will demotivate their current behaviour.

When you think about it, money is the most apparent form of extrinsic motivation. Organisations offer athletes millions of dollars; certain professions earn a decent salary and companies offer a relocation allowance. While money is tangible, there's intangible factors which drive motivation. Humans seek external rewards through praise, fame and public acknowledgement.

Extrinsic motivation has its use in different areas. If there's a reward tied to a task or outcome, you can be motivated to receive it. For example:

- Working for the benefit of receiving money
- Buying one item, accepting the other for free
- Using frequent flyer rewards
- An athlete transferring to a different team for the sole benefit of winning a championship

Our assumptions of what motivates others are regularly misconstrued. In the workplace, employers rely on an extrinsically motivated culture. Organisations work on the premise that staff are driven by reward and punishment. It's assumed that if teams aren't encouraged by receiving rewards and consequences, they'd have no enthusiasm or reason to work. The culture ultimately disregards other ways in which an employee can feel motivated.

For us to really appreciate what we do, we must be intrinsically motivated. This motivation, in its simplest form, is to do something enjoyable and interesting, without seeking external rewards. Intrinsically motivated people want to dictate how they work and provide themselves with some form of autonomy. Because they enjoy what they do, their rewards are internal and their actions are voluntary.

- For an athlete performing in their chosen sport, intrinsic motivation lies in their competitive nature and optimal performance.
- If somebody is looking to learn a new language, it's because they have an interest in exploring new things, not because it's a job requirement.
- If someone volunteers at a nursing home, they're doing something good for others which, in turn, brings the volunteer a full life.

- For an employer who allows an employee to pursue relevant projects, they do so because they're interested in encouraging growth and implementing guidance.

Although external rewards still remain relevant, we should be careful how much focus we have on them. Intrinsic motivation is gradually lost once confronted by a world that's heavily reliant on extrinsic rewards. As children, we're driven by internal desires to learn and discover. We observed anything and everything. But once we start to grow, we are programmed by society's demands and become more controlled in how we're motivated. If we get good grades, we go to university. If we finish our working week, we earn money. Slowly, we start to forget more and more of what we used to appreciate. On our journey to adulthood, genuine dedication to certain things decreases with age.

We're all different and behave in different ways. Our perspective of what's a reward versus punishment varies from person to person. Some of us are more intrinsically motivated by tasks and others see the same activities extrinsically. While both are effective in their own right, we should use external rewards sparingly to minimise their effects of lowering intrinsic motivation. External motivation shouldn't always mean a negative outcome. We can see the benefits of accomplishment when completing unpleasant tasks, but should be cautious about excessive rewards.

3 WAYS TO CREATE INTRINSIC MOTIVATION

We're confronted by a different type of motivation every day. To create long-lasting encouragement, we need to set up our environment to radiate internal rewards. You can foster intrinsic motivation in three primary ways: curiosity, challenge and recognition.

Curiosity. Be curious about learning and mastering a particular skill. Notice the discrepancy between present knowledge and knowledge you want to attain and think of what could come of that knowledge when engaging in some activity.

Give Yourself A Challenge. Challenging yourself helps you continuously work at optimal levels while staying consistent towards goals. A challenge closes the gap between boredom and achievement.

Recognition. Humans desire to be appreciated. When your efforts are recognised, satisfaction becomes a reward and provides a boost of intrinsic motivation.

While intrinsic motivation is the ideal method for long-lasting motivation and behaviour, there's a time and place for both motivational types. For example, a manager should use bonuses, commissions and prizes sparingly. Although they're an effective way to motivate a team, employees should still be allowed time and resources to explore skills and projects they are independently excited about. A sole business owner should work for the rewards they seek, but not exhaust themselves in the pursuit of extrinsic compensation. Taking the time to enjoy other aspects of their life to remain balanced and effective will bring clarity to their business.

These two types of motivations, often at the forefront of our careers, aren't necessarily reflected in how we live. How are you motivated? What actions have you previously performed which provide you internal rewards?

Your answer is a reminder to direct your attention back towards what matters to you so you can continue on the path of a rewarding life. When you recognise how you're motivated, you begin to structure your actions around your motivators. The direction of your life improves and you start to understand how you structure your actions. The same application not only exists in the workplace, but in everyday life as well. The hobby you start, be it learning how to cook or pursuing something that interests you, can be turned into a passion if you continue feeling the enjoyment it brings. The powerful motivation of a newfound passion encourages you to achieve certain goals—those which you become excited to explore and achieve with curiosity and without apathy. Once you begin to direct your actions towards what you appreciate, the trajectory of your life improves and you become autonomous in how you show up each day.

17

SETTING EFFECTIVE GOALS

Whether it's personally or professionally, goal-setting occurs every day of our lives. Goals start off as thoughts, causing us to think about the direction we take. Our thoughts can arrive on a smaller scale. For example, we want to show up to work on time or get out of bed early. Then there are those ideas we must double down on: buying a house, increasing our revenue, starting a family, etc.

Setting goals is an essential tool for motivation, self-confidence and happiness—creating a personal challenge gives meaning to your actions. When there's a path to follow, you become more self-aware of your behaviours and have a distinct road map which provides navigation tools to get you there. Goal-setting is a process that starts with careful evaluation and consideration of what you would like to expect from yourself. To achieve a desired outcome, some form of sacrifice is required. Larger goals often require the additional ability to develop an unconscious routine.

We are often told to find something we love and stick to it, yet numerous times we have taken action on the advice of others only to fall short. When we fail to achieve our goals, we think there is something wrong with our approach, or the goal itself. We create excuses: "If only I had more time in the day" or "I'll start tomorrow". The excuses we make generate clouded thoughts. Although it feels like a failure to set goals, the problem is often our ability to focus. To have clear thoughts during the goal selection process, you must choose a priority and eliminate the problem.

Do you want to wake up earlier? Eliminate going to bed at a later time.
Do you want to exercise more? Remove unhealthy foods to feel more energetic.
Do you want to write more? Take away mindless activities and set a time block.

The process of elimination when first setting goals naturally gives a burst of excitement and encouragement because there's novelty in what we're doing. We're excited to explore our newfound mentality. But our focus starts to diminish because we haven't been able to establish a clear pathway. When this happens, we begin to introduce what we first eliminated back into the equation. As I've previously mentioned, the biggest contributor to setting and achieving goals is having a simple yet effective system. Your systems provide guidance and help your decision-making, then building on relative habits enhances your ability to continue progressing.

The most notable difference in failure and success is knowing how to navigate through roadblocks that arise on any given day. When you understand your way around the threat of derailment, you begin to move forward with deliberation.

CREATE THE SPACE

My good friend, Kris, wanted to have the best-looking lawn on his street. The more he cut it, the better it performed. The more he invested in the grass, the more it grew. When lawns grow, they create unnecessary blades that make the grass look unattractive and unhealthy. Regular mowing helps build a healthy and robust root system, increasing the performance after each mow. If you want your lawn to thrive, you need to cut away some of the good and bad grass to fully develop the root system.

Our goals are similar in this way. As we grow, we want to achieve new things while still maintaining our current habits and lifestyle. For instance, we might want to exercise and eat well every day to lose weight, but our current lifestyle makes it almost impossible to sustain. While it may work well for a couple of weeks, it eventually catches up.

We need to cut down some of our goals and habits to create the space for our top priorities. Only then are we able to optimally perform and grow in what we seek to achieve. But the question remains: how can we set goals effectively?

Matthew McConaughey is a stellar example of redesigning goals to create valuable space. He wore many different hats at one point in time and referred to himself in one interview as a great "over-leverager".

McConaughey once owned a production company, was an actor for hire, a family man, owned a music label and had a foundation. One day his phone rang, and as he went to pick it up. He saw it was a number from his office and hesitated. Mid-reach, McConaughey let the phone ring out and questioned himself, asking, "Why did I pause to pick up a phone call from my office, where I pay these employees, and they do great work for me?" As soon as the phone rang out, McConaughey called his lawyer and said, "Shut down the company, shut down the music label. I'm making B's in five things. I want to make A's in three things. I want to be an actor for hire, I want to have my foundation and I want to be a family man".[1] He refers to making that decision as one of the best he's ever made because it allowed him to perform highly in the most critical aspects of his life. By having too many goals, he was unable to prove effective in what he valued most.

Use this example to question your own goals. Are the sacrifices you're making worth it? Are you willing to go through all the tedious work that comes with the process of achievement?

My mother represents this in all forms. In her forties, she had a goal to climb Mt. Kilimanjaro, the highest freestanding mountain in the world. The required training was immense and training twice a day was the norm. She had to be willing to go through altitude sickness, constant tiredness, soreness, fatigue and regular bouts of physiotherapy. Her acknowledgement of what had to be sacrificed ensured she was in the right frame of mind to succeed. She ultimately achieved the mountain climb, after which she took this mindset towards trekking the Kokoda Trail in Papua New Guinea six months later. And that's where it starts.

Rather than asking what kind of success you want, ask yourself what kind of discomfort and pain you're willing to go through. The easy part is to have a goal. Everyone wants to succeed in life—whether losing weight, being offered a promotion, building the right relationships or becoming a best-selling author—but nobody wants to suffer. In order to succeed, you must be ready to accept the dull, often mentally painful and tedious process that comes with an attractive outcome. When you gain clarity on your sacrifices, your system for achievement becomes much more effective.

STACK YOUR GOALS

I will [BEHAVIOUR] on [DAY] at [TIME OF DAY] at/in [PLACE].

"I will write every weekday at 6 am at Secondeli Cafe".

This specific, yet straightforward sentence is what helped me turn an idea into a published book. You are two to three times more likely to stick to your goals if you make a specific plan of when and where you will perform a goal-reaching behaviour.

In 2001, researchers in the UK worked with 248 individuals to build better exercise routines over two weeks.[2] The candidates broke into three groups. The first group was the control group; they were asked to track how long they exercised. The second group was the motivation group; they were asked to track their exercise habits and to read and consume motivational fitness material.

The final group had the same task as the second group; however, researchers advised the participants to write down and formulate a plan of when and where they would partake in exercise over the two weeks. More specifically, each member of the third group had been told to complete the following sentence: During these two weeks, I will partake in at least 20 minutes of exercise on [DAY] at [TIME OF DAY] at/in [PLACE].

After two weeks, the results arrived:
Group 1: 35% exercised at least once per week.
Group 2: 38% exercised at least once per week.
Group 3: 91% exercised more than once per week.

Interestingly enough, the second group who had motivational material barely increased their exercise compared to group one, who had none.

By formulating where and when you'll perform a goal-reaching behaviour, the likelihood of achieving your goal enhances. It also leads to a lingering question and a timely reminder: How much time-consuming motivational material is beneficial to your goals? Are you consuming too much information that prohibits you from taking action and progressing?

• • •

When setting goals, our focus tends to be on the minimum threshold we want to hit. For example, we say, "I want to exercise at least three times this week", or "I want to write at least a thousand words today". But benefits also arrive by way of sustainability and progression when implementing a maximum threshold in our goal-setting behaviours. For instance:

"I want to exercise at least three times this week, but no more than five".
"I want to write at least a thousand words, but no more than fifteen hundred".
"I want to make at least fifteen sales calls today, but no more than twenty".

Implementing a minimum and maximum target opens up the sweet spot of performance and progress. In many parts of our lives, there's an area of sustainable growth we try to reach. The recipe of growth is to make progress, but not too quickly that it becomes unsustainable.

In 2016, I set myself a goal to compete in my first boxing fight. I viewed the fight as the reward for all the hard work I put in. Low and behold, it didn't come to fruition. I quit right before I was supposed to get in the ring. At the time, I thought I was doing all the right things. I didn't have one drop of alcohol for six months. I became obsessed with training, heading to the gym twice a day. I solely focused on having a minimum output.

I hadn't set clear boundaries which essentially led me to exceed my output capabilities, leading to burnout and a loss of habit and routine. The mental and physical exhaustion drove me to fall out of love with the sport. I would suffer from the occasional mental breakdown, accompanied by the inability to get out of bed in the morning.

Some would say my mind was weak, and others would tell

me to try something new. But the way I see it, I lacked the knowledge of sustainable growth throughout the journey. Having a maximum threshold makes the process of progress much less complicated.

When you establish a routine, you start to understand what's sustainable and where you can start increasing your limits. The maximum threshold helps you show up each day while becoming aware of how you're progressing and growing.

We all want to get from A to B as quick as we can—it's human nature. But patience, combined with the consistency of small, daily behaviours is what's required to regularly achieve extraordinary things.

18

POWERFUL STAGES OF A PERSONAL CHALLENGE

Throughout our lives, we consistently build on our efforts to achieve something of value. Some value arrives in stages, like buying a car, building a house or getting a promotion. While other value arrives through our daily efforts: waking up early, eating healthy, going to the gym, etc. The flow-on effect from creating a personal challenge is potent. Over the years, we continue to examine our actions and set new and improved benchmarks for ourselves (consciously and subconsciously). Some we accomplish and others we fail miserably. But one of the most extraordinary things about consistently setting a target isn't just the ability and confidence to improve on the challenge itself, but in doing so, we simultaneously enhance other areas of our life.

On the quest to live a rewarding life, we go through five different stages: obtaining an inner belief, applying action, working through failure, becoming resilient and the feeling of accomplishment.

As you continue to strive, these stages will continue to present themselves. Understanding how to respond when they arise is vital. Let's go through each stage in detail.

• • •

Stage 1: Obtaining Inner Belief. Without belief, effective action does not exist. While action is the key ingredient to achievement, faith and trust are what ultimately get us there. Scientists once believed that humans would respond to information coming into the brain from the outside world. But over the years, research has found we react to our previous experiences and what we expect to happen next based on those past experiences.[1]

Our mind is a powerful tool. Positive expectation provides inner belief. For instance, if you want to lose weight or simply wake up an hour earlier, you must acknowledge that it's a choice and a discipline of the mind. The same applies if you're keen to leave your nine to five job in pursuit of freedom and independence. No matter how big our challenge may be, you're required to make a choice. The longer we sit on the decision-making fence, the less likely you are to jump off and act on what you seek.

To apply an inner belief, envision what a rewarding life looks like to you. Envisioning is not simply asking what success looks like, but delving further into what brings you energy and joy. You can then use your answer as a tool to reach the depths of what you truly desire.

When you visualise, you naturally create motivation, inspiring yourself to start believing. You then unexpectedly begin to take action, moving closer to achievement.

For instance, if you're seeking a promotion, you might find yourself taking on more responsibility and risk in your professional life. Or perhaps you visualise yourself in a new home and you naturally gravitate towards saving.

When you believe in your ability to perform under the challenges you create, your probability of achievement increases, encouraging your likelihood of applying the required behaviours.

Stage 2: Applying Action. It's often the case that we don't know where to start. When this happens, we get overwhelmed, pushing our thoughts further away from the action required. When there's an initial goal that becomes overwhelming, don't be afraid to outsource your route to make life easier.

- A person looking to increase muscle mass may seek a nutritionist to gain knowledge.
- A small business owner looking to build a website might hire a website developer.
- An employee looking to become a top-level manager might invest time and money in skills and workshops to reach their goal.

Taking action through outsourcing provides an outline in finding your optimal route to work through because we simply can't do it all.

Once we have direction in our actions, the road still won't be fully clear. To provide clarity in our efforts, we need to focus on two things: planned action and our daily habits. When planning certain behaviours, build them up as milestones. These milestones should be specific and relevant to the result of your goal. For example, how many times a week will you exercise? What steps in your business plan do you intend to take over the next three months?

When you've mapped out the small and steady steps, you're set up with a system that focuses on implementing the daily habits required to maintain progression. Think of your habits as a support network. They provide structure and routine, helping you accelerate your planned action. They're a way to invest and compound your efforts over time, leveraging your ability to manage stress and maintain focus. When you get intentional about what actions you take, you can use each action to your advantage.

• • •

Stage 3: Working Through Failure. Navigating our way towards a rewarding life brings many milestones. But we will undoubtedly encounter failure along the way. The solution to failure is in our ability to expect uncertainty and not turn away. Fear, perfectionism, distractions and a lack of self-belief are all logical reasons we fail. When these occur, we allow ourselves to stop taking steps towards our destination.

Have faith and remind yourself to shift your inner dialogue from "not good enough" to "more than enough". Work through failure by recognising it as a prerequisite to rewards and use it as a source of motivation.

We've been taught to believe that poor performance, impaired judgement and bad luck are the reasons why we fail. We link lack of success with the colour red (stop) and achievement with the colour green (keep going). In reality, we're stronger and more courageous when we fail. If we're not making mistakes, we're not learning. By shifting our perspective, our perceived failures can become one of the most powerful tools in making significant breakthroughs.

The traditional mindset within many organisations is to punish and penalise failure. The problem with this tradition is that it causes fear and stagnation in progress and creeps into our daily lives. For example, we may not hit our targets, so we don't get a bonus, or we haven't performed as well in a new role, so we get demoted. The fear of making a mistake triggers our instinct of self-preservation. The result causes us to shy away from experimenting and embracing the risks we take.

When we take risks, we tend to overestimate the chances of something going wrong. We heighten the downside of taking the risk and, in return, misjudge the outcome of a situation. The reality is, the likelihood of risk is often a far better return than we imagine. No matter the outcome, you grow throughout the process and become more resilient and confident in bouncing back from failure. Leverage your mistakes and make realistic assessments by reminding yourself there's still so much to learn and achieve. Your failures are a direct link in the chain of achievement.

Stage 4: Becoming Resilient. When you live through the downside of failure, control your emotions and experiment with new approaches, you garner resilience. Resilience is a skill because it's an adaptive mode of thinking that gradually improves over time. When you build durability, you're prone to taking more risks, thus improving the chances of achieving future success. We have two options when we fail: become self-defeated or become encouraged. While the latter is harder to do, perspective makes it easier.

Perseverance requires a goal, a passion and patience. It requires a personal challenge. The absence of resilience can predispose us to overwhelming conditions and place us in a feeling of hopelessness. When you fail, you learn to adjust and adapt to circumstances. Implementing new practices strengthens your capacity to demonstrate resilience and accomplish more. The bottom line: When resilient, you're more willing to accept new challenges thrown your way. You're able to manage the impact of adversity and through your experiences, you can achieve your goals.

Stage 5: Feeling of Accomplishment. When you think about it, we're consistently setting challenges and striving for personal success. We create plenty of milestones in our lives: we buy a car, get engaged, have children, get married, get promoted, etc. But what's it all for? Of course, it's the satisfaction and pride of personal accomplishment. But overall, we aim to live a rewarding life—one with direction. We aspire to make an impact on ourselves and others.

Achievements are not about the goal itself but the journey it has taken to get us there. It's the belief that turns into action, where our failures and resilience define who we are. Working your way through the maze of personal challenge brings out the best in you. Once you reach the goal you've set for yourself, take time to enjoy the view and give yourself credit for what you've accomplished. Use that time to recharge and reflect on your success and keep moving forward.

FIVE STAGE GOAL-SETTING PLAN

I know many individuals and have researched several others who have reached their goals. They all have one thing in common: there's an ultimate goal, whether it's to become an author, win a championship, run a six-figure business, or become an expert in their field. These people are the reason why we become inspired. Setting goals is a necessary process because it anchors the way we go about improving. To close out pillar three, I employ a fresh perspective of how you can set your goals —a system that aims to ignite a new, replenished desire for achievement. In reality, life without goals becomes aimless, a chore, and brings discomfort in day-to-day living. But when you have something concrete to work towards, you create purpose and open up the opportunity for remarkable rewards and ultimate satisfaction.

Many goal-setting books teach the value of having SMART goals (specific, measurable, achievable, relevant and time-based). In theory, it's a great concept because it's relevant to the outcome, but it also fails to bring total clarity in who we look to become. I've applied a five-phase process which connects your goals to your identity and gives you an action plan to sustain intrinsic motivation on the path to a rewarding life. The five phases are: connecting with your ultimate goal, defining who you want to be, setting a high end goal, setting a low end goal and designing your routine goal.

• • •

Phase 1: Connect With Your Ultimate Goal. To achieve your ultimate goal, you must be able to connect with it. Ask yourself:

Who do you want to be?
Where do you want to go?
How do you get there?

For example, being an entrepreneur, becoming an author or becoming a professional athlete are great "who do you want to be" goals. But they can't be reached without defining what route you will take and the strategy you'll use to get there.

This takes introspection of understanding your current environment and whether or not it's supporting the ultimate goal. Connecting your environment with your ultimate goal changes as you grow. It's important to adjust as you move along and not to worry about the finer details. For instance, your ultimate goal may be to switch careers, which requires new education. Your current environment with a child on the way and a wife at home makes your ultimate goal feel impossible. Rather than divert away from your dreams, audit your environment and engage in a plan that directs you towards your ultimate goal.

Phase 2: Who Do You Want To Be? What are your current constraints and limitations which hold you back? Reflect on your answers from a mental, physical, genetic and environmental point of view. For me, I struggle to focus for lengthy periods of time. In my journey to become an author, some days I would spend five minutes writing and other days I would spend an hour. I had to be willing to be patient and acknowledge that the five-minute days would add up over time, and there would always be another hour day. But more importantly, I had to understand and find common ground with my weaknesses. Defining who you want to be stems from the willingness to accept your weaknesses and build on them over time.

Do you want to be a successful business owner? Are you in

the right environment to help you succeed? Do you need to gain more knowledge and skills to reach your ultimate goal?

Do you want to be physically healthy? Do you need to build muscle or lose weight?

Asking these questions provides an understanding of the strengths and weaknesses you face so you can shape your identity with confidence and conviction.

Phase 3: Set Your High End Goal. Most of the time we set our high end goal without implementing the first two phases. It makes sense because the high end goal is more exciting and gratifying to daydream about.

The high end goal should be something that's completely challenging to you but that you still believe is possible. For example, my high end goal was to publish this book and my ultimate goal was to sell over one hundred copies. It's challenging, yet achievable. The more practise and work I apply, the more achievable it becomes. Without the belief of achieving a high result goal, we aren't able to navigate through the roadblocks and obstacles that come our way in reaching it.

Phase 4: Set Your Low End Goal. We don't always achieve what we set out to do. Setting the bar too high and consistently failing makes us feel like giving up and shoots down our confidence. Having a low end goal enables us to celebrate small wins while preparing for more. Your high end goal may be to lose 15kg. You might then set your low end goal at 5kg or an achievable target you're happy with. When you achieve this, the low bar gets raised again to something more achievable. As you continue to close the gap towards your low end goals and ultimate, high end goals, then your high achievement gets closer. A high target creates the desire. The low target keeps you on track to fulfil that desire.

• • •

Phase 5: Design Your Routine Goal. When setting goals, it's essential to understand what it takes to achieve them. The process goal is to do what's needed regularly enough to achieve your ultimate goal. In other words, low end goals are considered the habits within the routine we employ to help reach those goals. In the case of publishing this book. Getting it published was my high end goal. The low end goal was to write thirty thousand words. My routine goal was to write five hundred words every session. By doing this, a habit began to form and my routine had been put into place. Five hundred words became the habit and the routine, which allowed me to focus easier because I knew what I needed to achieve and had a system in place to get there.

Those that reach the pinnacle in their chosen field get there by practising each day and having a system that makes it easier to achieve their ultimate goal. The five-phase goal process keeps our eyes on the present and away from the future. You can't work in the future or change your past. Looking at the ultimate goal and thinking how far you have to go becomes overwhelming. Which is why it's important to take an approach that focuses on one single thing you can do now to make improvements over time. The five-phase process provides a pathway and the opportunity to connect a system to your ultimate goal. Each phase allows you to think and answer questions you may not have thought about in pursuing your goals.

19

THE PITFALLS OF GOAL SETTING

While setting goals provide an excellent way to create direction, our best intentions can cause us problems if we're unaware of what to look out for. For many years we have been told that to get somewhere, we need to create specific, measurable, actionable and realistic goals in our approach. I instilled this thought process for many years and took it as gospel.

I would set a goal on how much weight I needed to lose.
I would set a goal on how many words I needed to write.
I would set a goal on how many days I would go without alcohol.

The downside in this approach meant that the goal became the end game. It was something to be reached. The problem is, what happens after you get there? Do you stop doing all those behaviours that helped you get to where you are? I eventually learned that success arrives by the systems we have.

For example, an athlete's goal may be to win a championship. Their system includes how often they train, how they receive feedback from coaches and how they communicate with their team.

A writer's goal may be to write a best-selling book. Their

system includes how often they write, how they gather research and material, how they edit, design and format their work and how they market their book once published.

In these two examples, if you remove the goal from the equation and only focus on the system, what would occur? What if, as an athlete, they stopped focusing on winning a championship and instead focused on training often and communicating well with the team. Would they still get results? Yes, they would. Remember Olympic boxer Harry Garside from earlier? He did exactly that. That's how he became an Olympic bronze medallist in Tokyo after preparing most of his life for it.

The mind struggles to focus on an outcome that is seemingly far away when performance relies heavily on the daily priorities which support the outcome. While goals ensure direction, systems provide progress. The key is to not get caught up with the end goal but to focus your attention towards your systems instead. Progress and success will follow. Although it can be exciting looking forward to reaching a destination, we still need to be wary of the following two pitfalls.

Goals Can Prolong Happiness. We often have the mentality, "Once I reach this goal, I'll be happy". We assume happiness is waiting for us when, in fact, it should be with us every day. This is something I've fallen victim to. I used to think, "I'll be happy once I lose this amount of weight" or "I'll be satisfied once I get to the end of the working week". For many years, my future self was always waiting for happiness. Goals can also have the tendency to provide conflict. You either reach your goal and become successful or you fail and become a disappointment. Putting yourself in an all or nothing position narrows your happiness and restricts your ability to enjoy the process. Focusing on balanced behaviours provides the remedy to overcome an outcome and promote daily happiness as opposed to working to reach it.

• • •

The YoYo Effect. Having a mindset that focuses only on a specific goal can create a "yo-yo" effect. This effect is increasingly evident in dieting. Individuals would eliminate certain foods for a period of time, causing an imbalance in diet. When they give up halfway through or complete the goal, the individual quite often reverts back to old habits and they're back where they started. When you set goals, you set them to achieve the outcome. When you set your systems, you set them to continue performing the outcome. Focusing merely on a single accomplishment makes it challenging to sustain the work you put in every day. Your focus should be on the cycle of continuous improvement and committing to the process. A goal is great to have when planning, but your systems are what gets you progressing.

We often think goals are a foolproof way to help us get to the finish line the best way possible. But what we forget is that, if we aren't careful, our goals stop us in our tracks and we struggle to keep achieving what we set out to do.

There's been two major words you've encountered in pillar three: "system" and "action". While it's true that without goals we don't have direction, what's equally true is that without the right system and without applying the right actions, we don't see results. So far, pillar one looked at what's important to you. You asked questions of yourself that determined the direction you would take and were reminded to do something remarkable as opposed to being someone remarkable. It was a stepping stone that led into pillar two, which provided direction in understanding and making decisions best suited to a life that's rewarding to you. As pillar three comes to a close, take a moment to remind yourself of your goals. Ask yourself if you're performing the right habits that benefit where you're heading.

We often forget the value in understanding who we are and where we want to go. It's why we get stuck in having a goal-oriented mindset. Set up your system so you're in a position to apply what the next pillar brings: effective habits.

20

ACHIEVING WHAT YOU SEEK: SUMMARY

- Focus on building your identity based habits that align with who you want to become.
- When you break down your goals into small wins, momentum will be hard to stop. You can then work to practise patience and persistence as you continue on the path to achievement.
- Continually remind yourself there's still so much to learn and achieve. When you fail, think of those failures as a direct link in the chain of your achievement.
- Through tracking and measuring, you begin to understand how you're progressing. Progression is not just about results. It's about making sure you're on the right track.

PILLAR IV

DEVELOPING EFFECTIVE HABITS

"We are what we repeatedly do. Excellence, then, is not an act, but a habit". – Aristotle

As we reach the halfway point in the book, take a moment to check in with yourself on your decisions and the goals you make. Are your current habits in alignment with what you seek? How consistent are you? Are there any bad habits that halt your progress? The next pillar of living a rewarding life is about linking an identity to the habits you carry out. Without employing identity-driven habits, there's a disconnect between our direction and what's important to us. Throughout the following chapters, we'll look at the basic science behind your habits and how to build a positive relationship between your identity, your environment and the behaviours you apply as you continue on the path to a rewarding life. Your behaviours and habits ultimately define who you are and what you do. Without awareness of them, progress is limited.

. . .

Kieran Behan was born in Hertfordshire, London, in 1989 to parents of Irish descent. At the age of six, he fell in love with gymnastics and would watch all the summer sport events. Kieran aspired to be in the same position as his idols flipping through the air and landing on the beam. The hopes and dreams of one day becoming an Olympian led Kieran to begin practising gymnastics at eight years of age. The more Kieran showed up at the gym, the more he flourished, and coaches started to witness the exponential improvements he made at such a young age.

Unfortunately, after a couple of years in the sport, doctors found a tumour in his leg. He required surgery, and further complications meant Behan was wheelchair-bound for at least a year. After fifteen months of painful rehab at such a young age, Behan was ready to return to gymnastics. His passion was quickly rediscovered as he continually showed up to practise. But that once again changed just eight months later. Behan was practising a high bar routine when his hands lost grip. He smacked his head on the horizontal bar in what could only be described as a freak accident. The landing caused a traumatic brain injury and damage to his inner ear, losing all of his coordination skills.

Behan was once again refined to a wheelchair—except this time, he had to relearn the simple skills of sitting up and moving his head. It took two years before he could regain his hand-eye coordination and to stand up on his own two feet. As soon as he could stand up, back to gymnastics he went. It seemed the more Behan practised, the more adversity he faced. Despite these setbacks, he returned to gymnastics and achieved several awards as a Junior gymnast. In 2006, Behan finished fourth at the Junior European Championships in Greece. A milestone for the setbacks he had faced. Behan struggled with minor injuries in the years that followed, including a broken arm and a fractured wrist.

Following his success at the Junior Championships in 2009, he underwent ACL reconstructive surgery on his right knee. The procedure had a nine- to twelve-month recovery period. His focus was on recovering from the surgery and breaking into the senior ranks. But once again, his senior debut was put on hold as he ruptured his ACL in the other knee. Behan's spirit was being tested but still maintained one goal: to continue practising gymnastics. October 2010 was finally the moment he made his senior debut on the international scene, competing in Rotterdam's World Artistic Gymnastics Championships. He participated in three of the six events without dismounts due to recovering from his most recent ACL surgery.

At age twenty-two, 2011 became the breakout year for Behan as he competed in the European Championships in Berlin, winning gold, silver and bronze medals. The success led him to qualify for the London 2012 Olympics games' final stage—the last hurdle to achieve his dream. Behan didn't receive any funding from the Irish Sports Council of Gymnastics Ireland to compete in these competitions, which meant he had spent close to twenty-four thousand dollars on travel and accommodation. The support came from friends and family who raised money through bake sales and car washes. In the London Prepares Olympic Test Event, Behan qualified for the floor exercise final, finishing in fourth place but gaining the best execution score of the final. His performance booked him a spot in the London 2012 Olympic Games, becoming only the second Irish gymnast to compete in the Olympics. Although he was experiencing the best form of his career without injury, fate struck again. One month before the London Olympics, he broke the metatarsal in his foot. Despite the injury, Behan competed but unfortunately couldn't qualify for the event finals. In the following months of the 2012 Olympics, Behan underwent further knee surgery. Due to the tumour surgery as a young child, part of his left quadriceps muscle was removed—meaning his leg would never be the same.

After another long rehab process, Behan overcame resistance to compete in the 2014 Artistic World Championships in China, then again in the 2015 World Championships. It was the most competitive season in Behan's career, qualifying in the final stage to compete in the 2016 Rio Olympic Games. He earned a silver medal on the floor exercise and became the only Irish gymnast to qualify for two Olympic Games.[1] Unfortunately, Behan did not reach the final for any of his events due to dislocating his knee on the first tumbling line. At this point, injury was almost expected. He bravely carried on with the routine, defining how he has always lived life: with continual practise, purpose and intent.

After returning home, Behan underwent another left knee surgery, where he received devastating news. This time he accepted it. The Rio Olympic Games were his last competition as he needed a total knee replacement. Behan retired from the sport but still hasn't lost his love for gymnastics. He took his knowledge and expertise into the role of coaching, becoming the Head Junior National Coach of Austria.

As we move into Pillar Four: Developing Effective Habits, Kieran Behan's story can be viewed as a stepping stone into how you can show up consistently in the direction you take and overcome inevitable obstacles faced when taking action. The roadblocks along your journey are overcome not by our ability to be the mentally toughest and physically strongest, but by our understanding of developing habits and key requirements when navigating through difficult situations. If we're unable to continually perform actions dedicated to the type of person we want to become, it's difficult to achieve what we set out to do. For us to achieve meaningful results, we're required to perform what are, quite often, monotonous actions on a regular basis. Without knowledge of the basic theories and how habits shape our identity, we're unable to find the right relationship with who we are and where we want to go. This pillar provides that knowledge.

21

HABITS AND THE BASIC SCIENCE

As we navigate through the world and our stages in life, we're bound to come across multiple reactions to the situations we find ourselves in. Our conscious and unconscious reactions are targeted to meet our needs more effectively. Our ability to develop conscious behaviours are aimed at enhancing our life, while the unconscious behaviours are those we would potentially like to break. The habits we hold are often deeply ingrained in our brains, proving it a challenge to implement effective habits and remove bad ones. To understand how to implement good habits (and break bad ones), we need to strip back the paint and understand what enables our responses and why we keep repeating the same behaviours. If you're an avid reader of nonfiction and have read previous writings on habits, this information may be familiar. My aim is to not reinvent the valuable science made famous by Charles Duhigg and sensationally popularised by James Clear, but to remonstrate basic principles with effective, action-based approaches so you can make the right decisions and perform the right behaviours.

FORMING A NEW HABIT

For us to build any habit, there are three stages we go through: the cue, the routine and the reward. All three stages represent an important phase in the structure of our behaviour.

Stage One: The Cue. A cue gives our brain the signals required to initiate a behaviour, ultimately predicting our reward. The cue is essentially a trigger, leading us to respond accordingly. There are five primary ways a habit can be cued: time, location, prior event, our emotional state and other people.

Cue 1: Time
The most common cues come from the time of day. For example, waking up in the morning triggers a domino effect of habits. We go to the bathroom, brush our teeth, have a shower, eat breakfast and continue with our day. Our time-based cues can be used to stick to basic routines or rituals over and over again.

Cue 2: Location
Quite often, our behaviours are a response to the environment we surround ourselves in. For instance, the couch is a prominent location for mindless habits. It's familiar, and because we pair the couch with dinner, it's easy for us to mindlessly binge TV and snack until we go to bed. Because we have already mentally assigned our habits to our location, if we want to build a new habit, we need to overcome the cues our brain has predetermined to that area. The effort to shift location cues in our current environment requires more mental resources than if we were to build a new habit in a new environment, simply because we don't have to overcome any existing triggers.

Cue 3: Prior Event
Many behaviours we engage in are a response to an event we've previously experienced. These little events can be receiving a

notification which lights up our phone, having an extra glass of wine after a bad day or checking our emails after meetings. All of these habits are caused by preceding events which have triggered a behaviour. Our negative responses can be challenging to overcome in some instances because sometimes we have no control over the events presented to us. For example, how we respond to loss of job, death, injury, etc. can prompt self-sabotaging responses. However, we can limit these behaviours by adding an extra positive response to a specific event.

Cue 4: Emotional State
When our senses are heightened and we react impulsively to a situation, our automatic response tends to fill us with regret afterwards. Our feelings can be hard to control, and without sound awareness of our emotions, it becomes harder to respond to a trigger in a healthy way. We should think and assess what is happening around us. Although we are irrational by nature, to judge situations more effectively, reflect on past experiences and the decisions you have made during those experiences. How did you feel? Awareness is achieved through the conscious practise of analysing how you respond to your feelings.

Cue 5: Other People
Like our environment, those around us have the ability to influence how we behave. We can also influence how others behave. If we seek good habits, it's vital to surround yourself with those that have a positive effect on how you show up each day. If you're spending too much time with toxic, pessimistic people, their behaviours tend to sneak into your actions.

Selecting Your Cue. Before choosing your cue, review the five triggers and identify which ones are specific and readily actionable for you. Here are some examples:

Reading a book

Time > What time of the day? Will you read at 6 a.m., five days a week?
Location > Will you read in bed? Or on public transport?
Preceding Event > Will you read straight after breakfast?
Emotional State > Will you read only when you're feeling good?
Other People > Will you read only when a book is recommended to you?

Exercising
Time > Will you exercise in the morning or afternoon?
Location > Will you work out at a gym or at home?
Preceding event > Will you exercise after work or when you wake up?
Emotional state > Will you exercise only when you're happy?
Other People > Do you have friends to exercise with? Will they show up and work out?

Spending quality time with loved ones
Time > Will you commit to a set night/day for quality time? Is there a time of week which is easy to commit for both partners?
Location > Will the location be the same or different each time?
Preceding Event > Will you spend time together after exercising? Is there a preceding event that makes spending time together easier?
Other People > Will your quality time depend on one another? Will you communicate and commit to quality time with your loved one?

For us to be successful in selecting the most effective cue to change a habit, it takes some trial and error. A cue must fit within your current way of living. Once we are able to lock down a viable cue for a behaviour, we can then begin to implement a routine.

· · ·

Stage Two: The Routine. The mental and physical behaviours we take when presented with a trigger define our pattern. Although habits offer the same experiences in regular and repeated actions, a routine requires a higher degree of exerted effort. A habit is an unconscious thought performing a behaviour. A routine doesn't become a habit until it is automatic, and it only becomes automatic with enough time, routine and reward. It's important to note that routines vary not only in type but also in frequency. They may be fixed or flexible and are always being adjusted to succeed in evolving into a habit. One of the most challenging aspects in making a habit stick is to continually execute the routine right after the cue. This is where habit stacking becomes an effective tool. The term "habit stacking" was coined by S. J. Scott in his book *Habit Stacking: 97 Small Life Changes That Take Five Minutes Or Less.*

Habit stacking helps us smoothly transition from a trigger to a routine with consistency. The approach consists of identifying a current habit you do and anchoring that habit to your new routine behaviour.

"After [CURRENT HABIT] I will [NEW HABIT]".

Current Habit: After I brush my teeth in the evening
New Routine: I will read for half an hour.

Current Habit: After I get home from work
New Routine: I will clean the kitchen.

Current Habit: After I exercise in the morning
New Routine: I will make a smoothie.

Habit stacking is an effective strategy to implement new routines because we link them to a current habit pattern. When we link the two patterns together, it's more likely we will stick to a new behaviour because we are doing it alongside an action that's already consistent. But all of this is null and void unless we are receiving the right reward for our efforts.

Stage Three: The Rewards. A reward gives our brain an incentive to continue performing the routine. It's the final stage in habit formation, paving a neural pathway between habit and cue. But it's also the stage that keeps your momentum and motivation ticking at optimal levels. What we need to ensure in this stage is that the rewards we receive from our routine are both relevant to a desired habit and *actually* rewarding. They need to be satisfying enough to trigger your cue and routine. For example, I wrote the majority of this book in one particular cafe. Every morning at 5 a.m. I would wake up, drive half an hour, order a coffee and sit down to write for three hours. I received positive reinforcement each time I sat at the table to write, helping me stay motivated to wake up and drive the distance. More specifically, I satisfied my cravings for a morning coffee, activating my mind for the day, producing this book you're reading and missing peak hour traffic. Your reward can be anything which provides an end goal of every habit. Find a reward that will either satisfy you or teach you.

BREAKING BAD HABITS

Why is it that we can't rid ourselves of bad habits? We tend to do well for a week or two, and then we're back at it with the drinking, overeating and procrastinating. How is it that our best intentions are beaten nearly every time? We want to have good habits but almost always return to our old ways. The answer isn't our lack of mental toughness or not understanding what we want. It's that we don't know how to healthily deal with stress and boredom. The habits we have support our stress and boredom. They're known as our coping mechanisms. For some of us, these bad habits are caused by deeper issues. But if we want to make changes, we have to be honest with ourselves. Whether it's fear, limiting beliefs or personal past events, recognising our bad habits are crucial to overcoming them. Fortunately, there are ways to remove our coping mechanisms in an effective way; we can replace these habits with something that we know we should be doing. Because our bad habits have been ingrained in us, the hardest thing we could ever do is think about eliminating them straight away. All the habits we have right now, whether good or bad, are in our life for a reason. When we try to break a bad habit, we try to rewire our brain. The problem is, our brain is wired to enjoy habits, which requires a lot less mental energy than conscious decision-making, so it fights back against the idea of change. This is why the advice of "just stop doing it", which brings out the "easier said than done" response, rarely works.

Instead of eliminating a bad habit, we should replace it with a new one that fulfils a similar need. For example, if you drink when you get stressed, the idea is to not just "stop drinking". When stressed, you should come up with an action that provides a similar benefit. It could be going for a run or venting to friends. Expecting ourselves to remove the habit without replacing it will cause us to have certain needs that go unmet, which is why we revert back to our old ways after a week or two. Replacing a habit that provides a similar benefit creates a more sustainable routine long term.

REPLACING A BAD HABIT

There are four steps involved in breaking a bad habit: conceal your cues, make the cravings unattractive, make your response harder and make the reward unappealing.

Conceal your cues. Make your cues unseen. What triggers our bad habits comes in many forms. Our phone buzzing, driving past a fast-food restaurant or having a carton of beer in the fridge are all examples of what could be triggering our bad habits. If you're always checking your phone, leave it in another room. If you're always driving past fast-food restaurants on the way home, take a different route. If you have a carton of beer in the fridge, only leave a couple in. Breaking bad habits becomes easier once the cues are removed.

Make the cravings unattractive. Have you ever regretted staying out late after a big night? We've all been there. Too much alcohol, too much greasy food and a two-day hangover. We can make a late night less attractive if we schedule a morning workout session or an early morning catch up with a friend. Staying out late then becomes unattractive which makes us recognise we should go home earlier. If you struggle to eat healthily, joining a gym goes a long way to curbing your bad habit cravings. Being surrounded by people who take their health seriously makes us rethink eating bad food all the time. We are a product of our habits, thus we are a product of our environment. Breaking bad habits requires a support group who encourages us to be the person we wish to be.

Make the response harder. Bad habits form because they are easy to implement and give us the least resistance when we're bored or stressed. After all, why bother responding to stress and boredom by doing something more difficult? Breaking a bad habit can be made easier by increasing the amount of resistance associated with performing it. For example, if you have trouble snacking and eating too much food at home, clean out your pantry. Replace the bad foods with good foods. If you find yourself always checking your phone, turn off your notifications. Our bad habits are hard to break because they become too easy and convenient to live our lives. Increasing the steps it takes to make the process difficult makes it easier to rid ourselves of bad habits.

Make the reward unappealing. The final step in breaking a bad habit is to make the reward that's associated with the bad habit unappealing. Ultimately, our good habits are compromised by our bad habits. The cost of our good habits is in the present and the cost of our bad habits are in the future. For example, if you're eating pizza on the couch every night, the reward is a dopamine hit from the carbs and fat. Our brains aren't built to weigh up the long-term costs and short-term costs accurately, so we need to find ways to make our bad habits unappealing. In this instance, we can change our environment from the couch to the table. If you set the table before organising dinner, your mind is more likely to think of a different meal besides pizza. All of the sudden, you're more inclined to eat something healthier with a knife and fork because of the different location and environment you set up.

When you find yourself falling into a bad habit, stop and recognise how you will respond. Hack into your mind by concealing your cues, making the cravings unattractive, making your automatic response harder to take action on and manufacturing an unappealing reward. By doing so, you'll have a strong ability to break your bad habits and enhance the likelihood of replacing them with good ones—and ones you become satisfied with.

22

SHAPING YOUR IDENTITY

One of the biggest challenges we face when applying habits is to align them with our identity. It's often the case that our behaviours aren't a reflection of where we would like to be. We read for a couple of days, then don't touch a book for months. We go to the gym three times in one week, but skip exercise for the next six weeks. Inconsistency presents itself for two reasons: we're focused on the result, and we attempt to change our habits the wrong way. We go through three levels when turning a behaviour into a habit: the outcome, the process and the result.

When focusing on changing the outcome (level 1), the focus is solely on changing the results—for instance, being promoted, buying a house, losing weight, writing a book, etc. These are the goals you set for yourself. The battle we face is educating ourselves on a process which brings us closer to our identity. All we have so far is an outcome. The second level provides that essential link in turning our actions into consistent behaviours. Changing your process depends on the routines, systems and ideas you create when changing your habits. For example, you may book your gym classes in advance to promote your attendance. Most of the habits you build occur at this level, providing a gateway to who you want to be. Reaching the process stage provides a deeper understanding of your beliefs, views, self-image and judgements on yourself and others. When it comes to building good habits, the focus should be on the direction of change in our behaviour. When we start off, many of us build habits based on the outcome, or "what we want to achieve". But by considering our identity and "who we wish to become", we practise our habits from a place of evolution, shifting our trajectory in line with who we want to be.

Imagine two people who wake up at the same time each morning. When questioned why they wake up before sunrise, the first person says, "I try to wake up early each day". While there's no reason to question the response, the language implies this person hasn't yet tied their identity to their behaviour. When person two is questioned as to why they wake up early, they respond "I'm a morning person". The small difference in how they respond lets us know who they are, and who they're trying to become. Most of us, when attempting to improve, don't consider who we would like to become. We just think, "I want to wake up earlier" but we haven't considered our beliefs which drive our actions. If we're unable to shift the way we look at ourselves, we encourage our old identity to sabotage our new behaviours.

I want to wake up earlier (outcome).
I try to wake up early each day (process).
I'm a morning person (identity).

Among every system of action is a system of belief. Professional sporting teams routinely train each week with a belief of winning a championship or title. A writer sits down to write each day with a belief to publish a book. An employee shows up to work each day with the belief they will get paid. When a behaviour isn't aligned with our identity, it will not last. In the example of waking up early, if you're looking to get out of bed before sunrise but consistently go to bed late, you will continue to choose sleeping in over early mornings. The same goes if you seek exercise but continue to choose excuses over achievement;

your thoughts revert back to finding an excuse as opposed to going to the gym. It's difficult to change our habits if we are unable to connect our new beliefs with the behaviour.

Most of my life I didn't consider myself a writer. In fact, it wasn't until 2021 where I maintained a consistent publishing schedule, sharing articles on my website. When I became consistent, I took tremendous satisfaction in taking a step back and seeing the work that I had done and still had to do. I was proud. Since I began writing in 2018, I can say it's now embedded in my identity. If I miss a day, it feels unnatural. This book came to life from the small, consistent behaviours embedded over time. I was able to produce this through continual incentives that came from my habits lining up with my beliefs and who I wanted to be.

The ultimate form of effortless motivation happens when your habit becomes your identity. Once this occurs, you take pride in the behaviour performed and you're more motivated to maintain the associated habit. When your pride gets involved, you can channel your ego to continue on the path of doing something remarkable. The only way to truly change your behaviour is to change your identity. You might start a habit because of the inspiration you receive, but to continue it, you need to live with it.

Don't become someone who wakes up early, become a morning person.
Don't become someone who shares knowledge, become a coach.
Don't become someone who learns guitar, become a musician.
Don't become someone who writes, become a writer.

Once a person believes in a characteristic of their identity, they align their habits with what they believe. For us to begin to believe, we need to be satisfied with what we get back from our behaviour. Most of us expect to see results right away. We think, "I've been trying, but nothing's changing". What's occurring is that our old identity has taken over and we've let our outcome get in the way of progress. It's not only challenging, but exhausting when our old self takes control of who we are trying to become. To overcome this, it's important to understand how we can change our identity. We have talked about aligning our habits with who we want to become, but all that is null and void without understanding how to become who we seek. This leads us to a lingering question: how can I change my identity?

THREE QUESTIONS TO ANSWER

Whatever you tell yourself right now, that's who you believe you are. What you believe stems from the evidence which has stacked up to support it. If you wake up early each morning, you believe you are a morning person. If you continue to work overtime, you're dedicated to the job. If you exercise often, you're committed to training. Our identity and belief in who we are doesn't occur overnight. If you wake up early once, you wouldn't consider yourself a morning person. But if you wake up early on a consistent basis, the story you tell yourself begins to change. You start to think, "I'm starting to believe I'm a morning person". The only way to close the gap between your current belief and a new identity is through small actions that evolve over time. Those small actions evolve into small achievements, and then into a new identity. To take action on what's important and produce identity-changing habits, ask yourself three questions:

1. Who do I wish to become?
2. How can I get there?
3. How will I measure my success?

First, decide who you wish to become. In Pillar One: Understand Yourself, I spoke about our ego and our ability to coexist with what's important. Who you wish to become should align with what it is you do and who you do it for. When we focus on becoming a person with purpose and process, our values and beliefs work in sync with each other to begin shedding our old identity as we evolve into someone new. The person you wish to become develops by connecting your actions with small progress. It's at those small progression points where your beliefs start to change.

How we improve our life shouldn't be thought of as an overnight project but as an ongoing, systematic way to live. If the way we think works in line with our actions, how we get there becomes a much easier question to answer. It is the simple actions which keep us on the path of progression. When we consistently perform simple acts, the gap starts to close between how we get there and employing a new identity. While keeping in mind our new identity and goal, it's important to build up small accomplishments over the course of the journey. For example, your new identity may be to become a writer and your goal is to write a book. You achieve this by consistently accomplishing small tasks over time.

Identity: Become a writer
Outcome: Publish a book
Small Accomplishment: Write two hundred and fifty words each day

The final question we must ask ourselves is how we'll measure our success. I initially measured success as writing two hundred and fifty words each day. If I achieved this consistently, I was on track. The benefit of measuring small accomplishments is feeling successful when the action becomes easier. For example, two hundred and fifty words may seem difficult at the start, but over time it becomes effortless. When an action becomes easy, we should shift the goalposts and increase our measurement. Two hundred and fifty words may turn into five hundred words. Five hundred words turn into a thousand words and so on.

Success requires refining our measurement—continually measuring our progress against process as opposed to measuring achievements against the goal itself. Similar to how we implement high end goals and low end goals, we're creating a system for success. If we think of success in small achievements, we're not focused on how far we have to go. Instead, we become dedicated to the journey that takes us there.

Goal + Process + Small Wins + Measurement = New Identity

To keep your mind clear for action, focus on building identity-based habits that focus on small achievements so you become someone who achieves the outcome and identity you envision. To reach any goal, implementing smaller and more manageable milestones along the way is key. The small wins represent your progress points. They are what keep you moving forward and staying on track.

There are, of course, challenges we face when committed to developing a new identity. We become impatient, life gets in the way, we're uncertain, etc. In pillar six, I target overcoming these pain points while acknowledging that life does become challenging. We lose motivation, we struggle to stay on top of our mental health and we deal with unexpected moments. But we must build a solid foundation of action before we can overcome the pressures and demands of life.

23

THE RELATIONSHIP WITH YOUR ENVIRONMENT

Imagine you're at the shops, shopping for the upcoming Christmas season. The place is packed, and it's almost impossible to find what you're looking for. You decide to take a break for lunch and make your way to the food court. The plan is to order a healthy salad with a bottle of water. Unfortunately, the line at the healthy lunch spot is far too long for your patience to withstand, so you look around to see what else is available. There's a fast-food restaurant with a small line, leading you to weigh up the two options; do you wait in line for an extra five minutes to buy a healthy lunch, or do you line up and order fast food to satisfy your immediate hunger cravings?

Psychologist Kurt Lewin believed that forces drive our behaviour, similar to how physical objects are influenced by gravity.[1] Some forces come from within us, from our feelings, attitudes and goals, and this is part of what reflects who we are as people.

If you want to start exercising more, then that desire is a force that drives you to hire a personal trainer or join a gym. If you continue to work late and miss your scheduled exercise session, that would be a restraining force on your exercise goals.

Lewin referred to these situations as "environments". An environment is considered anything in the world that surrounds us—anything but ourselves. It includes the time of the day, the location we're in and even the current weather. These are the external forces that drive or restrain our actions. Lewin arrived at a conclusion which he refers to as the force-field principle. The premise behind the theory presumes we tend to stick to the status quo unless forces of friction or fuel push us in a particular direction. We can acknowledge, though, that behaviour represents a function of our environment. Each decision we make requires a trade-off and has the potential to bring unintended consequences. In the example of buying your lunch in a busy shopping centre, many external factors sway your decision: the number of people around you, what time you buy lunch, your mood when you woke up that morning, etc. These forces push you in a particular direction to make a specific choice.

Every day you are situated in powerful environments driving or restraining your desired action. Netflix is a timeless example. When a show ends, the next one starts automatically without you having to move a muscle. Similarly, when you purchase goods and services online, the company saves your information. The friction of buying is reduced because all other steps have been completed. The behaviour becomes more appealing because certain forces have made it easier to perform.

When we create new experiences within a new environment, they have a higher potential to become habituated. For example, lying on the couch to watch TV after a long day might give us a positive feeling of relief and gratification. But the more you do that action, the more your mind associates couch and TV with stress relief. There's nothing inherently wrong with this association. The problem with our repeated behaviours means we are prone to losing self-awareness through these environmentally triggered behaviours. There's a direct correlation between our environment and our emotional memories. Each time we repeat a behaviour, it increases its habituation pattern. Eventually, the behaviour establishes itself as a natural and responsive routine. Our environment is heavily influenced by the information we receive: television, phone calls, texts, notifications, updates, etc.

The constant stream of data can dictate our mood, time management and daily decisions.

The bottom line is, our environment can persuade us to forgo what we know we should be doing and replace it with what is easy. The question now remains, how can we set our environment up to prompt action and behaviours in line with what we seek?

The key is to make your habit cues more obvious. There are a few different ways to achieve this:

- If you want to read more, place a book on the lounge room table and beside your bed.
- If you want to exercise more, book your gym classes and set reminders on your calendar.
- If you want to start or finish writing a book, create a workspace you enjoy sitting down at.

To make something a big part of your life, the cue needs to be a big part of your environment. One of the most effective ways to turn a behaviour into a habit is to surround yourself with multiple cues. Think about the triggers which cause someone to compulsively check their phone. They could be bored, waiting to meet a friend, stressed or between tedious and repetitive tasks. The same approach can be applied to your good habits. If you're surrounded by triggers that help you take action on a good habit, it significantly increases the likelihood of employing the required practices throughout the day. Making your cues extremely obvious allows you to make easy decisions that are governed by your goals.

When you design or redesign your environment, you do something extraordinarily powerful. You become more in control of how you see the world and how you show up each day, creating a sense of freedom that otherwise never existed. Most people have their environment designed for them, leading to mediocre results. But those who are the architect of what they consume enhance their trajectory to achieve great things. Be someone who reduces the opposing forces surrounding your decisions and improves your exposure to your positive cues.

ENVIRONMENT SURROUNDINGS

When first implementing cues, they often start very specific. In the instance of reading more, putting a book by your bedside table will trigger you read before going to sleep. But over time, the habit becomes associated with your environment's conditions. Over time, you will *only* read when your book is by your bedside table. If it's anywhere else, you won't be inclined to pick it up. The trigger becomes part of your circumstances. We leash our habits to the location in which we perform them.

- We associate working with the office
- We connect exercising with the gym
- We link drinking with the pub/bar

How do you interact with what's around you? We establish our behaviours by the relationship we have towards our environment. For you, the study may be a place to get some work done. But for someone else, it may be a place to play computer games. Different people have different associations attached to certain locations—thus, different habits are practised. For me, the cafe became a reading and writing sanctuary. But for others, it was a place to converse with their children before school or catch up with a friend for breakfast. Even though we share the same environment, each with different meanings, we can teach ourselves a new habit in a particular context.

In a study that evaluated how classrooms impacted students' learning, scientists took photographs of thirty-five college classrooms and showed them to twenty professors and fifty-one undergraduate college students.[2] Each of them evaluated the friendliness and preference towards each classroom setup. Between 40-57% of the subjects based their evaluations on three out of seven classroom features: the view to outdoors, seating arrangement and seating comfort. The aesthetics of the classroom environment encouraged the subjects to attend school—thereby encouraging behaviour committed to learning. It's easier to change habits in a new environment. We can overcome the current cues and triggers that aren't serving our current habits:

- If you drive home from work and regularly order takeaway, drive a different route so fast food isn't an option.
- If you want to go to bed early, take the television out of your bedroom. You can also set a sleep timer on your living room TV to know when to go to bed.
- If you want to get more done at work, redesign the aesthetics of your study/office to create a fresh and appealing ambience.
- If you want to meditate, try the beach instead of your home.

When you remove yourself from your current environment where unhealthy triggers are activated, you leave behind a mental bias that no longer associates your surroundings with unrewarding behaviours. You then open yourself up for simple, unbiased action to create better and more rewarding habits.

While we can't always leave a current environment, we can rearrange it to achieve the same result. When I first started writing this book, I would sit on the couch and write. There would be multiple distractions affecting how productive I was. I then decided to turn my spare bedroom into an office. I bought a desk, bookshelves and office rug and made the location as appealing as possible to continue writing with zero distractions. I could then distinguish between "writing time" and "couch time".

What doesn't serve us well is when we mix the conditions of one habit with another. For example, you may have a work laptop and use it for personal use. But regularly mixing work habits and personal habits conflicts against the intended outcome. You will find personal use becomes easier to associate with the task because it's much easier to perform than doing work required of you. The key is to accommodate each habit separately. You wouldn't cook dinner in the laundry, and you wouldn't do your washing in your kitchen.

If you can consciously and regularly separate your behaviours to the location, you begin to think about your environment more objectively. Your thoughts make the action obvious because of your surroundings and it becomes easier to implement the proper habits and rid yourself of the unnecessary distractions. Just be sure to allocate and stabilise your environment so you can perform your desired actions by default.

24

STARTING SMALL

When growing a plant, we begin with a seed. We find a nice spot for it to grow. Once found, we begin to nourish the source so its roots are established and start to thrive. Forming a new habit is like growing a plant. We start with small actions, find a nice place in our routine to perform said action, and begin to nourish the behaviour so it's established in our life and grows over time. Early on in the process of developing a habit, we have a limited amount of motivation. The payoffs haven't occurred just yet, and we're still finding our bearings between using willpower and our automatic responses. The most crucial stage in habit development is the beginning, which gives us reason to ensure our behaviours start small.

Complex behaviours require a higher level of motivation, and because we're early in the habit development stage, we can't rely on motivation to perform and achieve results. One of the most basic examples we can compare a complex behaviour to is cleaning the house. You won't clean your house unless your motivation is high. But each time your home gets out of control, there's a dreaded feeling—a feeling of forcing yourself to act, of hyping yourself up to start cleaning. But what if your house was already clean and you only had two plates to put away? We wouldn't think twice about it because putting two plates away is significantly easier than cleaning two rooms.

As human beings, it's natural for our motivation levels to dip up and down over time in any particular behaviour. But relying heavily on motivation to create a habit doesn't work. Instead of using all our willpower, we need to start small. When a behaviour is easy to perform, we don't have to think about it. Simple acts like picking something up after dropping it or putting a book back on the shelf don't rely on motivation. For us to get results, we need to shift our focus to making our tiny behaviours automatic.

Think of how an Olympic swimmer achieves a gold medal. Their journey began when they first started swimming. They didn't simply wake up each day and break records. For years, they focused on the small actions required, building up to an Olympic moment. Athletes go through several habitual behaviours: waking up before the sun, recovering after a gruelling session, practising stroke technique, eating at the right times. These behaviours are what keep swimmers moving forward to achieve a dream. Yet when they first put their goggles on, they learnt how to swim with a kickboard—a small behaviour that started their journey to Olympic glory.

When we start small, over time our minds and bodies learn to work in unison, enabling us to consistently perform automatic behaviours. Our success comes from our small actions each day and is not necessarily a showcase of talent, but a result of dedication to the cause.

The consistency in simple behaviours compounding over time can produce incredible results. One thing to acknowledge when starting small is that simple is powerful. It's effective. Making a habit simple changes our behaviour and leaves us in good state to achieve results, allowing ourselves to keep motivation in the bank for when we *really* need it. But how can we accomplish this? How can we continue to build off small behaviours instead of burning through all of our willpower? There are three steps we can take to apply small changes and excel in our area of focus: start with an easy practice, increase in small increments and make repetition manageable.

Step 1. Start with an easy practice that you can't say no to.
I would write two hundred and fifty words each writing session a couple of times a week. It was simple, yet effective. After a couple of weeks, I could produce more. My capacity increased over time. I was building a capacity to handle a more significant habit of the same behaviour in the future.

For you: If you're looking to become more fit, start with one workout. Choose a time and location, perform the act and repeat until you notice improvement. Trial and error which habit you can perform that isn't difficult but that you can consistently maintain until you're ready to take the next step.

Step 2. Increase your habit in a significantly small way.
My word count increased to five hundred words each session and increased my sessions from two to three times per week. The minor adjustment mentally conditioned my capacity to endure five hundred words three times a week without a significant risk to performing the habit.

For you: If you are looking to increase your exercise, add in an extra day, but keep the duration of exercise in line with what you can consistently perform. Ask yourself, how can I increase my habit in a significantly tiny way to continue achieving results?

Step 3. Ensure easy repetitions.
I built myself up to allow a maximum of three hours of writing a day, five to six times a week. The word count was not the focus, the productivity in my performance was. Anything more than a few hours would feel too much and compromise other areas in my life. Rather than worrying about the outcome, I trusted that my work would improve through consistency over time.

For you: Once you have found the sweet spot of action and repetition, showing up starts to become automatic. When you've increased your habit the right way, it becomes easier to perform. You then begin to see continuous improvement with continuous results. The positive reinforcement starts to define your enjoyment of the process and your motivation remains at a high level.

When we take massive action, the fear of failure is higher, and so is the risk. But if you focus on the foundation of starting small, we begin to see compounded results over time. We naturally have limited patience for the small steps at first because of our need to see results right away. But that's when we should shift our focus to the present. Work on getting better at the small, daily actions. Practise showing up, and as you improve, you graduate to another phase of effort and repetition.

REAP THE RIGHT REWARDS

Up until now, this pillar has provided four key focus areas: the theory behind your habits, discovering who you want to be known for, assessing the relationship with your environment and the importance of taking action in small ways. Before establishing optimal performance in your arsenal, there's one question that remains: when, after all those repetitions, do you evolve into an individual who recognises and acknowledges the results you've achieved?

One of the biggest reasons why we give up early is because we underestimate how long it takes to get where we want to go and to become who we want to be. Applying repetition is not an easy feat. A 2005 study followed ninety-four members for three months at a newly opened gym in the U.K. to determine how people stuck to exercising. All ninety-four members paid the same membership fee and were all committed to attending. Out of the members, 29% used the gym consistently each week for three months. What's interesting is that the 29% who showed up weren't the strongest willed members (measured by their initial expression of commitment). They were still just as motivated as the other 71% who joined a gym. The 29% of people who persisted reported that they were in control of their exercise routine. They made their actions easier by reducing friction in scheduling certain exercise days. In the study's exit interview, the 71% started to see exercise as even more challenging. They reported a greater difficulty in attending the gym, thus increasing friction to exercise. For the consistent 29%, however, they grew into their new identity and couldn't wait to attend the gym.

When you make something a priority for a period of time, you're more inclined to carry the momentum through and continue on the path towards who you would like to be. Our priorities lead us to a new question: how long does it take to build a habit? Although a relevant question, what we should really be asking is, *how many repetitions does it take to form a new behaviour?* Applying a new habit should be looked at from a frequency perspective. Quite often, we view it through the lens of time, keeping us from focusing on the process and the simple actions required. To build any habit, you must practise it. Whether it's once a day, twice a week or a few times a month—the trajectory of your performance is directly correlated with your ability to repeat new behaviours. The best way to create repetition is simple: make it easy for yourself to perform a new behaviour. Similar to how we choose to make our triggers obvious, we must regularly put ourselves in the position to act without friction and doubt.

Uber successfully used the strategy of implementing obvious triggers to help their business expand. Wendy Wood, professor of psychology and business interviewed former head of economic research at Uber, Professor Chen[1]. Chen explained the difficulty in getting drivers to continue, saying, "The median driver doesn't last past ten trips. It's difficult trying to get drivers to stick around. That's always been the primary cost. There's just too many people willing to drive their own vehicle then there are more people to take a ride somewhere. It costs a lot of money to attract a driver. You've got to run a background check. Have a mechanic inspect their car. So I invest $1,000 in you as a driver, and you do only eight trips. I've just lost a tremendous amount of money".

It's clear that many Uber drivers associate their current behaviour with more friction to continue driving. Chen continued, "What's the barrier? Early on, it's a difficult task. It's socially awkward. A stranger is suddenly sitting in the back of your car and you've got to navigate that whole pickup, drop off relationship".

Uber changed the environment design of their drivers by employing a desired action to keep them motivated. Uber engineered a continuous pickup function; before the current trip ends, drivers already have their next trip lined up. The company had essentially created automaticity for the driver. Nowadays, instead of waiting around for their next trip, drivers can earn more money and create repetition throughout their day with an invested focus on their routine.

When you continue to perform an action, your experience of that action begins to change. You are no longer focused on showing up—your new focus is on performing well. What ultimately occurs is a graduation of experiences as you continue to break down friction with each repetition. When repeating behaviours, you stop consulting your intentions and continue to apply action.

Most of us repeat actions to become better individuals. We seek being better partners, better parents, a healthier version of ourselves, more productive and financially stable. Repetition allows us to enjoy those things more. Unfortunately, some of us are only interested in being fast-tracked to a new version of ourselves. It's why we fail in a relationship when we say we'll be better, but our actions prove otherwise. It's why we fail when we become too stressed and overworked in our career. While we underestimate our road to success, we also underestimate what we can do in a short amount of time. The power of frequency is a wonderful thing. If you're performing slowly and consistently, ideas remain fresh, the pressure is off and your productivity improves. What you do every day matters more than what you do once every now and again. When practising something new, you will slip up from time to time. What's important is to keep doing the essential behaviour until the act becomes automatic, requiring minimal effort.

25

YOUR REWARDS AND MOTIVATORS

Australian tennis champion Ashleigh Barty began playing tennis at the age of four. She had a promising career as a Junior, reaching a career-high ranking of No. 2 in the world after winning the girls singles title at Wimbledon in 2011. In Barty's teenage years, she had success on the doubles court with her good friend Casey Dellacqua, finishing runner-up at three Grand Slam events, all by sixteen years of age. In 2014, at age nineteen, Barty decided to take an indefinite break from tennis. She transitioned to playing cricket despite having no prior coaching in the sport.

Her interest was piqued when she met with the Australian women's national cricket team, where she spoke to the group about life as an international athlete. Immediately impressed by the team environment, Barty spoke with a Queensland cricket official about how she could try out and play, even having only played a couple of times in the backyard with her family.

Barty started training with the Queensland national league squad and top-scored in her first match with 63 runs off 60 balls. After the match, Barty said, "There's never a lonesome moment on the field if you're struggling. There are ten other girls that can help you out and get through the tough times". The transfer in skills was so impressive that Barty was selected to play for Brisbane Heat in the women's Big Bash leagues 2015 season. But by moving to a different sporting code, she had to make a significant financial sacrifice.

In 2013, Barty earned $600,000 for the year playing tennis. As a cricket player in the Women's Big Bash League, she earned $10,000. When reporters questioned the financial reduction[1], Barty responded, "Money was merely a 'side bonus' of being fortunate enough to play professional sport". Barty was then asked if she would make a comeback to the women's tennis circuit. Wise beyond her years, she responded, "I'll see when I'm twenty. It does look very glamorous on the outside. There are a lot of hours and a lot of sacrifices you have to make to achieve your dreams as a tennis player. It was tough being the only female player about my age. It was tough when you are by yourself."

After more than eighteen months out of tennis, Barty returned in 2016. Success almost immediately occurred. She won her first title at the Malaysian Open, rising to No. 17 in the world and went on to become World Number 1 in 2019 after winning the French Open. She then continued her impressive form by winning Wimbledon in 2021 and the Australian Open in 2022 before retiring at the top of her game.

What's impressive is that Barty wasn't receiving the rewards she hoped for during her first stint on the tennis circuit. It took a significant adjustment to find what she was seeking. Barty realised camaraderie and shared success was the key for her to grow as an athlete and a person. Ashleigh Barty's tennis triumph is a timely reminder: the habits you perform need to be beneficial to your identity. When you feel success and alignment in your identity, the brain tells you the habit is paying off and is worth the effort.

You and I are different from machines. A computer program would run through endless repetitions without being tired, whereas our patience dwindles quickly. We get tired of doing the same thing over and over again. It's why we need to profit from the habits we've applied.

Your environment paves the way for your actions, the repetition helps put one foot in front of the other and the rewards encourage you to repeat the habit. Rewards are not confusing, nor should they be. But what's often seen as straightforward and simple has a complexity behind it. If you can grasp the body of knowledge behind rewards, it creates a new thought process when applying a new habit that otherwise wouldn't have existed.

Rewards have to be more appealing than what you would normally experience. Imagine you're looking to implement a different activity with your partner each week as part of a weekly date night. You're in a happy relationship, but you're both seeking a little more variety in spending time together. For this habit to work, both have to exert more thought and creativity than suggesting the regular movie night at home. You both decide to put a new date idea into a jar, one date for each letter of the alphabet. Every week, you pull out a new date idea. The anticipation of pulling out an unexpected new idea creates a reward in itself. The size of the reward communicates to your partner the current standard of variety in the relationship. If you picked out a movie night for this week's date idea, it may be significantly less rewarding than last week's date of playing tennis because a movie night is usually what's expected every weekend. Unexpected rewards create a burst of dopamine to our brains.

Think about how you feel when you receive an unexpected care package at your doorstep rather than knowing a package will be waiting for you. Dopamine is a neurotransmitter and acts as one of the feel good chemicals in our brain. It interacts with the pleasure and reward centre of our brain and plays an important role in our feeling of happiness. Healthy dopamine levels help you seek and repeat pleasurable activities, while low levels can have an adverse effect on your psychological and physical well-being. When the brain doesn't receive dopamine, your motivation drops and behaviours and emotions start to become affected.

To achieve the right rewards from the habit, your brain needs to release enough dopamine to send a signal back, encouraging repeat action. In the example of you and your partner, it works like this:

1. Your partner's brain registers the new date idea with a release of dopamine.
2. The brain records and responds to the reward, allowing continuation of the weekly date night.

With repetition and continued processing, dopamine energises behaviours that ultimately lead to your goals.

What rewards can you create that encourage better living?

26

DEVELOPING EFFECTIVE HABITS: SUMMARY

- The roadblocks which appear along your journey are overcome not by your ability to be the mentally toughest and physically strongest, but by how effective your habits are and if they integrate with your passions and what you seek.
- If you begin saying "I get to do this" rather than "I have to do this", the story you tell yourself begins to change. You then start building towards the identity you seek.
- When you remove yourself from your current environment where unhealthy triggers are present, you leave behind a mental bias that no longer associates your surroundings with unrewarding behaviours.
- If you're performing slowly and consistently, ideas remain fresh, the pressure is off and your productivity improves.

PILLAR V

OPTIMAL PERFORMANCE

"No great thing is created suddenly, any more than a bunch of grapes or a fig. If you tell me that you desire a fig, I answer you that there must be time. Let it first blossom, then bear fruit, then ripen". – Epictetus

In 2014, Leicester City Football Club was promoted to the English Premier League division after spending five years in the lower leagues. As is the norm when new teams are promoted into the toughest football division, the club spent all season fighting relegation, hovering on the bottom side of the table. There was a predictability about it. A team would get promoted, only to be relegated the following season. No team in Premier League history had been at the bottom for as long as Leicester City (one hundred and forty days) and avoided relegation. It was at that period when a story so unlikely emerged through the depths of relegation, where consistency, systems and performance became the crux of one of the greatest sporting feats in history.

During the 2014-15 season, Leicester City went on a winning streak, earning victories in seven of their last nine matches. Football fans called it "The Great Escape", cementing Leicester another season in the Premier League and finishing fourteenth. It was a cause for celebration for the club. In the off season, Leicester toured Thailand, organised by late owner Vichai Srivaddhanaprabha. The outing unfortunately turned out to be an embarrassment for the club and owners when three players were accused and found guilty of racially abusing and exploiting female escorts in Bangkok. The Leicester board agreed to sack the players involved, as well as the coach, Nigel Pearson. Tasked with finding a new manager, Leicester found Claudio Ranieri after a swift search—an ex-Chelsea manager who they believed could bring Leicester out of their public relations turmoil. Ranieri's appointment wasn't well-received by media and pundits, who thought his best management years behind him.

That perception began to change once the 2015-16 Premier League season started. Leicester City had a new manager and the team was once again up against the likes of Manchester United, Liverpool and Arsenal, three of the biggest powerhouse teams in world football. Throughout the season, while the big teams struggled, Leicester remained consistent. They were written off to even make the top half of the table, but they were sailing fearlessly into the unknown. After every win, Ranieri consistently downplayed the possibility of winning the league. "My chairman said 40 points, 40 points please, then after if something happens it's okay, but 40 points", Ranieri said. For Leicester to earn 40 points in the Premier League season, it would sit them towards the lower end of the table, but above relegation. Leicester was exceeding expectations.

At that stage, top clubs and their supporters believed Leicester's winning ways were simply leftover luck from avoiding relegation the previous year. But that wasn't the case. Players earned confidence through performing courageously on the pitch. Their brand of football wasn't defined by one or two individuals. Leicester couldn't afford the best in the world. How they played came from realistic expectations and a belief in performing in a systematic, deliberate way. It came off the back of making less changes throughout the year, with Ranieri only making twenty-seven team changes in the season, compared to his recent average of ninety-four. Leicester relied on analytics in their recruitment process, employing a diverse range of players on the pitch. Although Leicester was top three in having the least amount of possession, for each opportunity they had, they converted the highest amount out of any other team. There was no secret to how they played. Other teams knew they would dominate Leicester on the pitch. Even Leicester knew that. But their ability to play to their strengths and perform in a systematic way eventually got them to the top of the Premier League. Leicester finished the season an incredible ten points clear of second place Arsenal.

When you type "5000 to 1 odds" into Google's search engine, the story of Leicester City F.C. comes up. The same odds to that of finding the Loch Ness monster and Christmas being the hottest day of the year in the U.K. The total value of Leicester City's squad in 2016 was £161 million. Second place Arsenal's squad was valued at £457 million.[1]

It serves as a reminder: you don't need to be the most talented or have the most expensive tools to perform and achieve what you set out to do. Remind yourself that no matter what you're up against, your ability to perform relies on belief and an effective system to perform simple actions. From there, you create the momentum required to achieve the results you seek.

I always used to think about what it would take to start writing. Would I be any good? Is it worth it? Over the years, I've come to understand one thing: effort, trust and consistency will *always* exceed talent. It's not about achieving everything right away; it's about setting up longevity in our actions so we can produce incredible results over time. To excel in any area, you must strive for small, continuous improvements. When that becomes your focus, you create more *valuable* time in your day and you begin to excel because your focus is aligned with importance. Then, you begin to open up an improved and efficient way of living with an understanding of what it takes to perform at your peak.

27

INITIAL BELIEF

When I first started writing, I would imagine having over fifty articles published, an achievement at the time which felt so far out of reach. I would continuously take "writing breaks", losing all motivation to seek new ideas and simply sit down and write. Never in a million years would I think to create and publish the book you're reading. Of course, I had dreams to become an author. But like many of us, those dreams lacked direction. When I found myself inconsistently performing the act that would keep me on the path, I had to change how I believed, and what I believed in. I made the error of thinking too far forward and not focusing on the small, daily requirements. I had to rewire my brain to believe that process and performance eclipsed results and rewards. I had to *fall in love* with improvement and not the end destination.

My belief came from curiosity and applying small-scale, basic actions. I would show up each day and write, acknowledging that not today but someday I'd have something to show for my actions. Some days words flowed. Other days I could barely get a paragraph out. But it was the small actions of showing up and not placing high expectations of myself to produce the most words or structure the perfect sentence that counted. My curiosity to publish a book combined with an expectation of simply showing up each day, no matter how effective I would be, provided the belief and motivation that I could produce something of value that would be available to anybody in the world.

When we start to see results from our small achievements, we naturally begin to do things unexpectedly, moving us closer to where we want to go. Consider your first small action to show up each day. When creating a belief, we shouldn't pressure ourselves into performance because it's easy to become overwhelmed. Rely on basic behaviours so you can advance through difficulties as momentum begins to grow.

There can be a lot of self-doubt and overwhelm before starting something new. Imagine this scenario: Anthony has applied for a job, and the company has called him in for an interview. He finds himself sitting in front of a panel. His anxiety and nerves are building. He attempts to answer all of their questions in a clear, confident manner, even with a little bit of humour. The interview ends and Anthony thanks the panel for their time. Walking back to the car, he's running through the answers in his head, trying to figure out if they liked him or not. Anthony is overcome with relief when the interview's over, but he still lingers in the unknown of whether he landed the job. A few days later, the company gives Anthony a phone call offering the position. He accepts and starts his first day the following Monday.

When Anthony arrives, the beliefs and feelings he had from the job interview are entirely different. He has started a new job with the confidence he can perform and achieve results for himself and the company, but there are now new feelings. What if Anthony doesn't get along with the people he works with? Will he still enjoy working for the company? The scope of his feelings shifts, and because he is still moving into the unknown, there is a form of nervous energy present. The doubt and lack of belief presents itself in the beginning because Anthony is moving into the mystery of performance. But as he shows up to work each day, his internal belief becomes more potent, and performance and achievement replace his initial feelings.

This example of self-doubt can be a reminder for us all. To set a new goal or start a new skill, we should remove the interview panel and co-workers from our imagination and just begin. Think of it this way: A rookie turned professional might have nervous energy when entering the pro ranks, but there's always a belief that they can perform well in a new environment. The beginning belief they possessed before becoming a rookie encouraged them to continuously improve their craft over time. If you want to start lifting weights, seek out a personal trainer. If you want to start cooking, print out a recipe and see how it goes. Perhaps you want to start writing but don't know where to begin? Put your imagination on a page and see where it takes you. Action is a fundamental part of progress and without it results are hard to come by.

Belief also requires us to use the time we have to our advantage. Before we start to learn a new skill or practise an improvement area, we should know when and where we will apply this action. This reiterates a valuable point: In order to improve in any scenario, you're required to understand the environment you put yourself in. What time of the day will you perform a behaviour? What will the scenario be? Where will you practise? When you prioritise action beforehand, you eliminate the excuse of not finding the time. From what seems like a barrier to begin, we open up the opportunity to improve. The most significant difference between those that perform and achieve their desired results and dreams and those who don't isn't intelligence or access to resources, it's the trust they have in themselves to find a way. The belief to make small and big things happen. Some of us trust in ourselves that we will move forward and figure it out and others believe the ideas and practices presented to them won't work. We need a willingness to experiment, think differently and find a way, even when feeling uncertain.

Although we can demonstrate belief within ourselves, we all experience times where we struggle to start. When we create the right environment and focus on the small, continuous improvements, our belief starts to compound. It is only then that our confidence builds and we can nurture our ability to continue practising. In some capacity, we all believe we are going to excel in life. It may be through a promotion, starting up a business or learning a new skill. But where we often fall short is when the idea of what it takes to excel contradicts our reality. We believe that *only* hard work is required. While hard work is necessary, we forget we have bills to pay, a family to look after, friends to see, sleep to catch up on and an overall life to enjoy. Before allocating our time towards what we envision, we need to again ask ourselves, is what I'm doing today helping me tomorrow?

WHEN WE STRUGGLE TO START

Why is it when we start something new or pick up where we left off, that endeavour doesn't last very long. We often say to ourselves, "Next week I'll start eating healthy" or "Starting tomorrow, I'm going to wake up earlier". We can liken our motivation (or lack thereof) to moving a heavy rock. Static friction is initially present, requiring us to use more force to start moving. When we finally get it off the ground, dynamic friction keeps the motion going. And because static friction is always higher between two surfaces, more forces are working together to resist movement.

Like moving a heavy object, when starting something new, it's a challenge to get going. Waking up early can be a challenge. Not working so late in the evenings can be a challenge. Eating healthy foods can be a challenge. Whatever we struggle with, static friction holds us back. When a behaviour becomes a habit, we do that behaviour subconsciously. When we start a new behaviour and contemplate the action required to begin, more friction is present.

So, what makes it harder for us to get started? For the most part, we let our motivation get in the way of progress. We strive to solve a challenge all at once instead of starting small and working *into* a routine. There are a few logical instances where this occurs. It's well documented that contestants on *The Biggest Loser* exercised for four to five hours per day. It's almost impossible to sustain that kind of effort in the real world, which is just one of the reasons why contestants struggle to adopt a healthy life upon return.[1] For the contestants, although motivated, they had to unlearn their behaviours and gain a new motivation relative to their everyday reality. Another example is an employer who requests their staff to work hours of overtime, causing burnout. The consistent work required of the employee becomes unsustainable, and they become disgruntled, seeking out a different job. The money no longer becomes worth the lifestyle risk.

Or perhaps we might learn a new skill on the weekend and spend all day practising, only to go back to work on Monday and never return to it. Rather than consistent practice, we try to learn it all in one day. By the time the weekend comes around, we have forgotten what it is we were working on, so we give up.

What's in our head is quite often different from the actions that help get us where we want to go. We lack the knowledge of being deliberate in practice and consistency. Instant gratification can negatively affect our desire to make transformations and get started on something new. We need to create balance so our transformation becomes consistent.

When we were younger, we performed habits we still have today: brushing our teeth, putting our seatbelt on, packing clothes away, etc. Our parents often gave us reminders. Actions that required prompting and thought became small, habitual actions. Starting something new or revisiting something old requires a small change that the brain can quickly learn from and repeat. We should break down our desires into daily behaviours. A powerlifter may plan to deadlift 300 kilograms, but they cannot achieve it unless they steadily increase their weights over time. Typically, we use motivation and willpower to keep ourselves going. But those resources only last so long. The small, daily behaviours last a lifetime. We should aim to connect them with a change in lifestyle.

For example, we may want to buy a house close to the city. Buying a house is life changing, but saving five hundred dollars a month is a lifestyle change. Starting a business requires the same mindset. The start-up is life changing, but promoting products or services becomes a lifestyle.

Having something to reach for provides direction; our actions determine our reality. Focusing too much on life-changing goals tricks our mind into taking on more than we can handle. What would happen if one day the powerlifter could only lift 100 kilograms but continued to attempt 300 kilograms? There would be too much static friction to get the weight off the ground, not to mention the increased chances of fatigue and injury. This is a reminder to focus on the small, daily behaviours required to keep us improving. Over time, the small wins add up and we continue to improve. The starting struggle we had became the past and the heavy rock of our performance is now moving at a steady pace.

28

HOW TO PRACTISE

"Women can't succeed and become an expert in practices requiring spatial thinking".

This is not a quote, but an old-age attitude present in 1976 before two Hungarian educators, László and Klara Polgár, decided to challenge the world's stance. Through the power of education, the Polgár's set out to prove that anybody could succeed and become an expert in all dimensions of thinking. The Polgár's homeschooled their three daughters while teaching them how to play chess. Being taught at a young age, their systematic approach to daily practice paid off. By the year 2000, all three daughters were world ranked in the top 10 of female chess players. Judit, the youngest daughter, was the youngest champion at fifteen years of age. A remarkable feat, considering the competition she was up against. Their approach to how they practised over time proved that results are achieved when the attention to perform is direct and specific.[1]

Gender differences aren't the only assumptions that have been shattered in recent times. In 1985, education psychologist Benjamin Bloom examined critical factors that contribute to talent. Bloom looked at one hundred and twenty elite performers who had won competitions, awards and international recognition in the fields of math, art and neurology. His research found no early indicators that could have predicted the success of the performers. Further research showed no correlation between an individual's IQ and their expert performance in areas such as music, chess and sports.[2] The only changes that proved significant (primarily in sports) were height and body shape. If the correlation of gender difference and different IQ levels does not affect being an expert in our field, how do ordinary people do extraordinary things? Through deliberate practice. Blooms' research and studies found that the performers' volume of quality was vital in becoming an expert. All performers he investigated practised with intent, listened to feedback from coaches/mentors, were students of the game and had consistent support throughout their developing years.

When engaging in deliberate practice, we should seek consistent, sustainable progress. The aim is to reduce the amount of time trapped between learning plateaus and improvement so we are able to perform as effectively as possible. There are, however, different practices, namely, naïve practice that contributes towards our inability to break through learning barriers. Naïve practice can be simply defined as practising and spending the majority of time learning in your comfort zone. Engaging too heavily in this form limits your true performance because the habits that are established aren't connected to an ultimate goal.

Examples of naïve practise might include playing a sport with a friend, practising music we already know or writing with no vision. Although we're performing actions and we see slow improvement, the progress doesn't last due to a lack of thought process in refining and upgrading our skills. Research from deliberate practice expert Karl Anders Ericsson found that once an individual reaches a level of acceptable performance and automaticity, the additional years of practice don't lead to improvement.[3] Also, if a practice is continually automated, it doesn't lead to continuous improvement. When we continually perform, over time we have the tendency to become caught in a loop which brings us back to being naïve in what we do because we hit a roadblock.

For us to break through plateaus, we need to take one step back and implement purposeful practice. We can then give ourselves the focus required to upgrade and improve our skill.

- In naïve practice, we're simply serving the ball. In purposeful practice, we're serving the ball into the top corner of the service box twenty times in a row.
- In naïve practice, we're teaching students. In purposeful practice, we're engaging in extra professional development work to become a leader.
- In naïve practice, we're going to the gym. In purposeful practice, we're tracking consistency and progress.

Purposeful practice is the reason why we see professionals and experts in their craft who are satisfied with their performance. They are constantly refining and upgrading, finding new ways to improve. When we become great at something, there's a tendency to become naïve in our performance, which is why we should practise with intent. When we do something purposefully, we attach specific goals to the action that requires our full attention. We should base our focus and thoughts on improving as opposed to the performance itself. This rings true in our basic life skills. If we focus on improving our communication, we can talk to others more effectively. If we practise making better decisions, we become better off. If we hone in on where we spend our time, we become more productive.

For us to continually advance, we need to attach relevant information to our progress. We require a feedback loop of improvement so our future behaviour edges us closer to our potential. Although we are more than capable of providing a self-assessment and not engaging a coach of some form, our evaluation of our improvement is likely to be less precise than someone else's evaluation. Our mind tricks us into a bias of wanting to reach our peak quicker when, in reality, we are further away. Mind confusion can ultimately bring us back to the beginning, where we lack motivation and that rock becomes harder to push. Be confident in asking questions and turning to someone you can trust, someone who has a mutual understanding in your endeavours. Athletes have coaches, musicians have teachers, entrepreneurs have mentors and employees have managers. Our ability to break through real and perceived barriers requires a secondary voice, one that recognises where our improvement areas lie.

During purposeful practice, there will be barriers to overcome. We may struggle to get past the next threshold that requires us to problem solve. For us to break through, we can perform different actions to reach the same results. For example, a weight lifter may struggle to reach a 100 kilogram deadlift. Instead of continually attempting the 100 kilogram lift, they may increase their reps at a lower weight to improve their form, then naturally progress to reach the 100 kilogram target.

When we reach plateaus, purposeful practice increases our ability to problem solve and focus in a different, yet effective way to break through performance barriers. When it comes to deliberate practice, and for us to improve on any level, we're required to leave our current experiences behind for a leap into the unknown. Coaches continually push their students to explore what's unfamiliar. The difficulty of being a coach often lies in changing the individual's mindset and encouraging the unfamiliarity of risk versus only seeking reward. To effectively exit our comfort zone, we need to find a compelling reason why. This involves taking the time to understand what we're practising, what's required for continuous improvement and visualising long enough to create momentum and trust within ourselves. Who we learn from provides us with the tools to improve, but only if we provide the actions. When it comes to truly defining deliberate practice, we can see it as performing with a purposeful and systematic approach with focus. Ericsson defined the concept admirably in his book *Peak: Secrets from the New Science of Expertise*:

We are drawing a clear distinction between purposeful practice—in which a person tries very hard to push himself or herself to improve—and practice that is both purposeful and informed. In particular, deliberate practice is informed and guided by the best performers' accomplishments and an understanding of what these expert performers excel in. Deliberate practice is purposeful practice that knows where it is going and how to get there.

When we practise deliberately, we show up proactively, looking to improve each day. We harness the ability to recognise mindless repetitions and engage in mindful practise. We shouldn't define our goals by how much we practise, but *how we practise*. Regardless of where we choose to direct our focus, deliberate practice helps us maximise our potential. Further practical examples can help us comprehend *how* we can practise.

Steph Curry. Leading up to the 2021 NBA season, Brandon Payne, Steph Curry's basketball performance coach at the Golden State Warriors, believed that making shots was no longer good enough. He knew that Steph was always going to make shots in practice, so they relied on technology to improve. Each time Curry hoisted a shot from the three-point line, technology tracked the arc of the movement. If the ball failed to drop in the exact middle of the ring, it was a failed attempt, even if he still made the shot. It was a mental challenge to try and be as perfect as possible. As it stands, Steph Curry has the most three pointers in NBA history.

In Combat Sports. It's common in combat sports for athletes to employ different types of coaches. An athlete may have a striking coach, a conditioning coach and a nutritionist.

The striking coach focuses on boxing and strategizing performance.
The conditioning coach focuses on priming the athlete's physical condition.
The nutritionist focuses on fuelling the athlete so they can perform at their best.

On writing. A writer who wants to become an expert in speed typing would not practise writing a book to improve their speed. Similar to how a 100-metre sprinter would not run a marathon to become the fastest runner. A writer would time themselves regularly in short, sharp blocks of time to perform optimally.

Throughout the years, overall performance has improved. We see it in the Olympic Games, with athletes consistently breaking world records. Some of these improvements come from new equipment and rule changes. For example, the shoes that sprinters wear today are considerably more advanced than fifty years ago. The change in shoe technology has allowed for improved results over previous years. In 1904, at the World Typing Championships, the fastest typist wrote eighty-two words per minute. The speed rose to one hundred and forty-seven words per minute in 1923—an 80% increase in performance. [4]Since 2022, the record is two hundred and sixteen words per minute. The reason behind the improved speed is linked to advancements in technology such as keyboards, computers and new type speed measuring software. The fastest time at the 1986 Olympic Games marathon was just one minute faster than today's required entry-level into big event races like the Boston Marathon. And even when Russian composer Tchaikovsky asked two of the greatest violinists to play his violin concerto, they refused, deeming it unplayable. But today, elite violinists consider the concerto a standard performance piece.

In all areas of performance, knowledge, technology and

insights are continually advancing. We have access to more information and resources for improvement than ever before.

But the criteria for maximal performance will forever require deliberate practice. To master excellence in our chosen field and to fully understand the continual advancements, we require feedback. Without feedback, we reach plateaus that are hard to break. Similar to coaches providing feedback to their championship team, we should seek input in the field we focus on.

We don't need a significant amount of motivation to apply deliberate practice. We just need to know what we're passionate about improving and to ask ourselves if we're willing to apply time and energy dedicated to the practice. Once this vision is clear, we begin to understand the habits around us that are currently useless, noticing a shift in perspective, thus building up motivation to practise. Once we've engaged in this mindset, our focus then transitions to 1% improvements that compound over time. Deliberate practice gives us the road to progress, where the 1% keeps our energy and reason to perform at a high level.

29

THE 1%

During World War II, there was rarely any time or resources to allow for significant modifications in war equipment production. Instead of promoting significant and drastic changes to achieve desired outcomes, a USA war service (known as the Training Within Industry Program) recommended that organisations introduce small improvements to their progress. They were seen as continuous improvement initiatives designed for daily implementation. The essence of the method was predominantly used for improving the use of the existing workforce and technologies.

The continuous improvement initiative proved to be a success and saved the US manufacturing industry from a huge downfall. Post-WWII, economic reform took over in Japan where the US invited the Japanese to visit manufacturing plants in their country. Upon return, the Japanese took the successful concept and adapted it into what's known as "Kaizen"—the Japanese word for continuous improvement. Automotive manufacturer Toyota is one of the top companies today that uses this philosophy and applies it to their processes.[1] While the Kaizen method was initially set up to help businesses and economic reform, we can use it as a reminder that small, consistent daily improvements are how we can better our skills every day in our chosen area of focus.

- A writer doesn't get 100% better overnight. They get 1% better each day to reach their full potential.
- An athlete doesn't get 75% better overnight. They get 1% better each day to reach their full potential.
- A musician doesn't get 50% better overnight. They get 1% better each day to reach their full potential.

The Kaizen philosophy bases itself on our ability to make small improvements over time as opposed to significant changes overnight. The 1% gains are incremental. More often than not, we set ourselves a target to reach but attempt to make giant leaps to reach that target in the quickest time possible. Theoretically, reaching an ultimate goal as quickly as possible sounds like a great idea. But practically, it has the potential to produce burnout, fatigue, failure and feelings of disappointment. Slightly adjusting our everyday behaviour and habits focuses our mind on the 1% where we can make incremental improvements.

While an inundation of information can skew our thinking into trying different ways to improve every day, we should recognise the progress we make often lies in the simple solutions which come from our small actions. If the improvement is to read more, the solution lies in setting a time and location to perform the act consistently. If the improvement is to see family and friends more often, the solution is our ability to maintain communication and attention towards them. Progress often lies in the underwhelming, simple solutions.

Another strategy we can employ is to look backwards. When we set goals, we are attempting to predict our future. Opposites attract, and if we measure our progress in a different direction, we make decisions on what has already happened instead of what we want to happen. By measuring only where we want to get to, we're likely to lose motivation and effort quicker because we realise how far we have to go. When we measure backwards, the connection between what has already happened and our daily progress gives us the mental capacity and acknowledgement to either maintain our improvements or adjust them and keep progressing. It results in building off from what has already been accomplished.

- In fitness: Last week's lift was 90kg, so try for 95kg this week.
- In money: Saved $200 last week? Try and save $220 next week.
- In business: Sold only 10 products this week when the average is 12? Do five more sales calls next week.
- In relationships: Lacking quality time? Aim to schedule dinner once a week with your partner.

Measuring backwards is a gateway to making small improvements each day. When applying this strategy, we vividly imagine what behaviours we can apply today to make progress tomorrow. A goal worth setting is also a goal worth measuring. Continuous improvement is steady progress. Small progression points are not designed to change your life overnight, but over time, measuring goals effectively becomes an incredibly useful way to live because we build resilience, become empowered and unlock potential that brings us closer to our desires. The 1% progress we make each day is how we stay consistent and limit frustration, burnout and lack of progress.

30

ENERGY AND PERFORMANCE

As we get older, we experience ever increasing demands in our work and personal lives. We often respond by working longer hours, reducing physical activity and limiting time for our own improvement and self-care. Over time, burnout costs our ability to consistently perform at a high level, contradicting the reason why we respond to the demands in the first place. We disregard what ultimately fuels our capacity to work: our energy. Time is limited, but our energy is not. Tony Schwartz, founder of The Energy Project, helps organisations around the world limit the demands of extra hours and teaches them how to invest more in themselves to perform at their highest. Most employees develop the knowledge and skills in a position, but very few help educate and enhance an employee's capacity to perform. Yes, having more knowledge and skills often enhances the possibility to get more things done, in less time and at a sustainable level. In 2006, Schwartz and his team took one hundred and six Wachovia bank employees (now Wells Fargo) at twelve regional banks in southern New Jersey through a curriculum of four modules,[1] each focused on strategies to strengthen a particular dimension of energy:

Dimension 1: Physical Energy. The amount of energy we have, where we refuel through sleep and rest.
Dimension 2: Emotional Energy. How do we feel about what's going on in our lives?
Dimension 3: Mental Energy. The focus of our energy. Are we doing one thing at a time?
Dimension 4: Spiritual Energy. How the energy we expend makes us feel. The feeling we get when we expend energy that's more significant than ourselves.

Each module was delivered at one-month intervals to senior and lower-level managers and each person was assigned a fellow employee for support. Using Wells Fargo's key performance metrics, Schwartz and his team evaluated how the participants performed compared to a group of employees from the same bank who did not go through the training. The results were measured on a year-over-year percentage change. On a measure called "The Big 3" (revenues from three different loans), the participants who engaged in the energy modules showed a 13% increase in their year-over-year results in the first quarter of study. On the revenue for deposits, there was a 20% increase for that same quarterly period. The gains varied month by month, but the participants continued to outperform the group who did not go through the training. Although these results are based on the energy and performance of working in a bank, they are also applicable to how we live.

Schwartz undertook a study of Steven Wanner, a partner at Ernst & Young. Wanner was once perpetually exhausted, working twelve- to fourteen-hour days and finding it difficult to engage with his wife and four young children each evening. He slept poorly and made no time for exercise, eating less than substantial food. Wanner's primary energy-draining behaviour was constantly answering emails from the time he woke up to the time he went to bed. Reflecting off the energy modules, Wanner created a ritual of answering his emails only at specific times of the day. Before creating this strategy, his main concern was that clients or colleagues would see him as unresponsive and that he could possibly miss urgent messages. To address these concerns, Wanner extended an away message explaining his emails would be addressed at certain times of day and if something was urgent to call him. He also contacted each of his important clients to explain the reason behind this change. The new ritual meant Wanner was able to clear his inbox each time he opened it, expanding his ability to maintain attention on one task at a time. Interestingly enough, hardly anybody called him. The results of this simple ritual provided exceptional results. Wanner created valuable energy in his day. It produced a chain reaction of other small behaviours. He went to bed earlier and, as a consequence, was well rested and motivated to exercise. He lost seven kilograms in two months and was able to spend more quality time with his family. Although Wanner still works long hours, he focuses on one thing at a time. The difference is that he's now capable and aware of how he can renew his energy throughout the day.

Like most rituals, the key to results is specificity. If we don't satisfy each level of energy, we struggle to maintain focus, which hinders our ability to excel in the actions of our choosing. We need to look after our physical health, eat well and get enough rest. We don't have to be athletes or dieticians, but we need to find where we can improve and start building from there. Our physical energy supports all other energy dimensions. Without it, we struggle emotionally, mentally and spiritually.

When we're hungry, we can become agitated and aggressive. Conversely, when we're tired and need rest, we lack focus. Emotional energy is simply being in a healthy state of mind and not being held down by negative feelings. The emotions that don't result directly from our physiological state can help or hinder our ability to perform. Positive feelings like joy, interest or challenge increase our engagement and energy. Alternatively, bitterness, anger, sadness and all other negative emotions crush our energy. When we're overcome with these types of emotions, it's hard to focus.

Emotions aren't things we consciously choose. Sometimes we're upset for no reason, or we're anxious when we know we'll be fine. Feeling good is essential to doing good. To feel good, we have to let go of negative feelings, which we achieve by not lamenting the inevitability of failure or hurt, but by thinking about how much we can learn and grow. The majority of what happens in life is neutral. It's neither good or bad. We can make the choice as to what events mean in our life. Letting go of negative emotions and being grateful for the positive parts of our life is what provides us happiness. The simple truth: when we're happy, we have more energy.

Mental energy is where the focus of our energy goes. Sound mental energy is taking control of our thoughts as opposed to accepting the first thought that comes to mind. We should focus on using our mental energy to our advantage, using our mental muscles and skills to create happiness, focus, confidence, productivity and willpower within ourselves. The most crucial aspect in building our mental energy is entering into whatever thought we choose with optimism. When we begin with a negative outlook, we presume we'll fail. The way we think affects how we perform. If we're confident, we demonstrate confident behaviours, enhancing our likelihood of success. But if we aren't trained in willpower or have low physical and emotional energy, our ability to be mentally ready becomes tougher and decreases our ability to perform. Healthy routines and focusing on one thing at a time enhances our mental capacity to perform, leading us to connect with our spiritual energy.

Spiritual energy helps us understand what's truly important in our lives. For example, a person who values friendship would make more time for friend engagements. That person would seek activities and effectively maximise their time, experiencing high energy levels when investing their time with friends. Unfortunately, the high demands of a fast-paced world don't leave us much time to pay attention. We become blinded by this pace, unable to see meaning and purpose as a source of energy. We can use the corporate world as an example of this. We get frustrated with office politics, pointless meetings and staring at a computer screen all day, only to come home exhausted, to simply do it all again tomorrow. To truly find what's meaningful to us, we need to experience value in our created rituals. Only then do we start to see that attentiveness in our work dramatically influences how we perform. Our meaning and purpose are found in established rituals, where our behaviours and actions provide a source of positive energy and happiness. When we're doing what feels important, we experience a strong motivation to keep going. We feel proud, validated and grateful for our achievements in our work.

Energy is the battery for all our thoughts and behaviours. Being aware of how we can distribute it effectively helps us perform at our best and improves our understanding when we're exhausted. Our energy dictates when we need to rest so as not to risk burnout, but simultaneously our energy ensures we are challenging ourselves and pushing our limits towards increasing our performance and staying true to what's important in our lives.

PEAK PERFORMANCE AND FLOW

What happens in the bodies and minds of those in their fields when performing at their best? Mihaly Csikszentmihalyi once said, "Flow is completely being involved in an activity for its own sake. The ego falls away. Time flies. Every action, movement, and thought follows inevitably from the previous one, like playing jazz". Ask yourself: what do I feel when I'm performing at my best in an important area of my life?

The ultimate goal of performance is to exercise control over our consciousness rather than let external factors dictate our actions.

Modern-day language describes these experiences as being in a flow state, in the zone, in rhythm, in the groove, etc. When this occurs, our senses are heightened, and time feels like it has slowed down. We sync perfectly with the task, then action and awareness become effortless momentum. This state of performance is accessible to anyone who voluntarily pursues it.

When we direct our attention towards the activities we're passionate about and immersed in, we significantly increase our ability to improve. The more consistent we are in dedicating ourselves, the feelings that would otherwise consume us (fatigue, doubt, inhibition) begin to reduce. When we're challenging ourselves with an activity or task, our mind reaches peak capacity. And if this materialises in something we enjoy, we achieve a mental flow state, leaving us fulfilled and motivated to continue.

There are three different elements which contribute to achieving a state of flow and happiness: relaxation, goal-setting and connecting action with awareness.

Relaxation. In any field, relaxation is necessary to reach optimal performance. A violinist would posture up correctly and breathe to reduce the tension through playing. A boxer would learn to stay calm in the ring to avoid expending unnecessary energy. A parent would understand when they need to emerge from high-energy demands to refocus and re-energise. Performance anxiety is prone to inhibit peak performance.
Before engaging in an area of focus, we should practise being in a tranquil state. We can achieve this in different ways: exercise, meditation, performing at our optimal time of the day, etc. When we perform optimal behaviours from a tranquil state, we are able to remove ourselves from an overcrowded mental space, honing in on what's required. Our improvement multiplies because our focus does not provide room for external factors.

Goal-Setting. Without direction in our actions, it becomes hard to continually perform at our peak. When we set goals, we set ourselves up for deliberate practice, which encourages us to project our efforts into challenges. Knowing where we're at and the steps we need to take is essential to reach our goals. In return, we can measure our improvement effectively, helping us realise what's required of us when showing up to perform. In a flow state, we know what needs to be done. For example, a writer knows what topic to write on at any given time. A musician knows what notes to play. A doctor understands when to refer a patient and to whom. We all set goals, but learning how to understand our relationship with them is equally important.

Connecting Action and Awareness. Distractions in our daily lives are imminent. The friend attempts to have a conversation with someone but can't help notice what's occurring over their shoulder. The employee sits at their desk to work but finds themselves moving around the office on other matters. We all have, and will continue to experience little moments like these. In a flow state, our concentration is focused on one act, only aware of what is relevant to us in the moment. If the friend focuses on what's occurring elsewhere when having a conversation, they may miss a key piece of information. If the employee continues to move around the office unnecessarily, they risk 'busyness' as opposed to the more efficient 'productivity'.

Peak performance and flow are exceptional focus on what's in front of us and where we *should* direct our attention. To tip the scale in favour of the act, we should practise living in the present.

We should set an intention before each activity and start identifying our moments of focus throughout our day. The benefit is a significant increase of mental discipline to focus on our performance, relieving us of our usual fears that cause anxiety and internal fears of executing at our best.

The essence of peak performance and flow is not characterised by subjective feelings, but by withdrawing interference from our thinking mind. When a tennis player is dominating, hitting winners from any area of the court, they are not consciously thinking, "how can I get this ball past my opponent?" They are letting effortless momentum guide them. Their previous experiences in learning and performing creates space for unconscious action.

Being fully immersed in a worthwhile task indicates an absence of self. American psychologist Martin Seligman once said, "You go into flow when your highest strengths are deployed to meet the highest challenges that come your way". This is applicable in the work we do, the sport we participate in, the relationships we have and the life we live.

31

PRODUCTIVE LIVING

In economics, productivity measures the output per unit of capital, labour or any other resource, and calculates it as a ratio of gross domestic profit (GDP) to hours worked. Productivity is the essential source in economic growth; the improvement in standard of living is almost entirely dependent on the country's ability to produce more goods and services for hours worked. Since productivity is vital in an economy, it's equally essential in our performance. We often confuse ourselves by getting more things done as quickly as possible when the real task should be getting the important things done more consistently. For us to perform at an optimal level, productivity is measured in the efficiency to complete a task. No matter what we have going on, there are only ever really just a couple of important things we need to focus on at any given time.

Being productive is about consistently maintaining the same speed on what's crucial. For example, is the stay-at-home parent who spends most of their day changing nappies, cleaning up after their child and running errands all day any less productive than the parent who continually puts in overtime hours back at the office? For far too long, the metrics skew towards effective 'busywork' instead of what's meaningful and effective in life. The parent who works in an office may be extremely productive in producing a significant output, but the daily commute, the workload the manager places on them and the consistent extra hours may counteract their productivity. It can leave them questioning whether or not the tasks, hours and day-to-day pressures are of great importance. Meanwhile, the stay-at-home parent, although they face daily challenges as a parent, battling constant tiredness, they have their daily routine of cleaning, feeding, planning and self-care that fosters a healthy environment to raise a child in. It's a life filled with importance, and one they wouldn't trade.

For us to live effectively, we're required to design our environment and surround ourselves in ways which promote continuous improvement. The way in which we live ultimately comes down to two things: who we see and what we experience each day. We never live or work in isolation. We are consistently influenced by others and our surroundings, where attitude, health and performance shape who we are and who we are becoming.

What is one thing you can do where everything else would become easier or unnecessary?

How can you organise every area of your life around it? That one thing may be a change in your health habits or it may be taking up a hobby that can generate opportunity and income. No matter if you're an employee, parent, a business owner, an athlete or someone who wants to improve their performance to create optimum, meaningful work, understanding what's truly important is crucial. It requires time away from all the noise and allowing yourself to think and ask questions.

Start with the question that will now be familiar: *What is important to you?* Are the sacrifices you currently make justifiable? The required output in personal productivity is working on what's essential. We may be highly productive people and produce a lot of output, but can we distinguish the importance of our results and define if they're useless? When we focus on the right type of output, we get the right things done. Our results compound and improvements become evident in the areas we've chosen to direct our attention towards. We become more in tune with our behaviours and actions.

For us to ultimately improve our performance, we're required to align our thoughts and process in approaching what we do. We should face our current challenges and seek innovative solutions that assist us in the future. Similar to how organisations are required to evolve over time with their business models, individuals are required to do the same in their own lives. It's easy to get caught up in a monotonous way of living, where we ignore added stress, believing it to be part of the territory of living. But we all have choices available to us. Whether it's personally or professionally, implementing daily tasks and goals lies in our ability to gain a productive mindset. We often achieve half of what we want to set out to achieve and lack the motivation to continue. There is no light switch when it comes to maintaining focus and staying effective. Unfortunately, it's not something we can turn on and off. Our brain struggles to run smoothly. We should work to connect our minds with our performance through relaxation, goal-setting and awareness of our actions. We can then find flow in our performance and manage the ups and downs of producing significant work more effectively.

Research at the Chicago Consortium of School Reform analysed children's behaviour from kindergarten to university and how they react to the challenges of exams, stress and the nature of an academic environment.[1] The results showed three mindsets that influenced how students overcome the daily pressures they face. First, the students believed they would succeed. They believed they were "good" at a particular field of study. This confidence in their success was more predictive of their actual performance rather than any measured ability. Second, their confidence and ability grew with effort. The students understood the brain as a muscle. By showing up and consistently putting in action each day, they were motivated to learn and master their work. Third, the students valued what they did. For academic subjects to delve into the students' consciousness, the work needed to mean something. Students valued tasks and topics that connected in some way to their lives, their future pursuits and current interests. When a task was not valued, students expended more energy in mindless thoughts, resulting in less information stored.

Like children and teenagers, adults struggle to become focused and productive when the mind is absent from the task. We become useful in the easy work, but shy away from the hard work, leaving a bridge between what we want to achieve and achieving it. By valuing what we do and believing in our success, our confidence and ability will grow. That stays true in our work, hobbies and all aspects of life. So how do we achieve this? The answer sits deep in how we approach the actions that lead to our goals. Without understanding what behaviours are required, our productivity will be similar to that of a hamster on a wheel, consistently trying to catch and reach efficiency. To identify our focus and desired outcome, we need thoughts and a plan. For example, our focus may be to improve fitness in the gym. How will we reach this? What strategy and steps are required to help us apply the actions necessary? How many times a week will we deliberately practise the behaviours that get us from A to B? When bringing clarity, there are a few steps to take, designed to put us in a formidable position so we can activate the daily efforts required.

Step One: Identify A Prime Time. We all share twenty-four hours in one day, but not all of them are created equal. We go through productivity peaks and troughs throughout the day. While some of us require a morning coffee to get us going, others may require an afternoon caffeine hit. Some of us may be night owls and others are up before the sun rises. Identifying when we get our best work done helps limit the tendency to procrastinate and reach optimal efficiency. We should become aware of when our energy levels peak and when they dip. Pinpointing when we perform best begins with conscious recognition of our behaviour.

For example, I have set times of the day for certain behaviours: I write first thing in the morning, which is when I'm more focused. I then head to the boxing gym which helps relieve the mental buildup I've used when writing. My mind is then clear to work throughout the day, then in the evening, I have dinner and spend time with my partner. Finally, before I go to sleep, I'll read for fifteen to thirty minutes.

I make each behaviour I consider, important work for me. I've seen the ultimate value in setting my days up like this because I know when I do my best work. When we apply consistent behaviours when the time is good for us, we are rewarded by compounding results.

Step Two: Develop a Routine Before Your Day Starts
We're often told to wake up early, have cold showers, read, meditate, etc. In theory it makes sense. We should perform actions which bring us clarity and an overall sense of positive energy. But if our routine doesn't support what's important to us, our actions become useless. We should design our life so that the sequence of habits leads us towards doing the most essential things. When we apply this design, we send signals to our brain to take action.

One of the challenges we face in life is showing up each day and performing on a consistent basis. When we consciously think about what behaviours we plan to perform, we wake up with an understanding and motivation to achieve what's necessary that day. This conscious thinking results in managing mental fatigue because the decisions we make require less effort. If you want to exercise in the morning, set the gym clothes at the end of the bed. If you want to read more, put a book on your bedside table so you're more inclined to read. Preparation offers savings in time. And just like a bank account, with each deposit of savings, more time becomes available to us. The idea of developing a routine is to bridge the gap between making decisions and using our willpower. One extra decision made is one extra dent in our willpower.

Step Three: Self-Care

Putting extreme pressure on ourselves to perform inevitably creates a physical and emotional toll, where distractions rise, engagement declines and energy decreases. The key is to manage our energy levels, assess when we're performing well and when our energy levels drop. In a 2019 study, The National Library of Medicine showed that student nurses are much more likely to neglect their health and well-being while learning to take care of others, reducing their effectiveness in providing care for patients.[2]

Scheduling time for self-care and realising when we require recharging is essential in getting the important things done. For optimal performance, taking care of ourselves is vital. We need to use it in a way that doesn't compromise the time we spend on tasks. Developing a sleep routine, aiming to eat healthy, taking regular short breaks and taking time for what you enjoy are all ways to benefit future efficiency when in focus. We should aim to use these at the right time so we can re-energise and focus.

These three steps represent a blueprint for building a foundation and mindset for productivity. Having a consistent base fosters better performance in the actions required to improve and reach a goal. The key is to not let time and resources dictate what's best for you. Once this happens, you're limited in your ability to consistently show up and improve. If there's something of high value that you want to achieve, beat your time and resources to the punch and take control of how you spend your day. Use your prime time, routine and self-care as a platform to create daily actions. These actions become habits, and those habits become small wins. Those wins add up and over time, and success will arrive.

32

OUR ABILITY TO PROCRASTINATE

Throughout history, humans have always been putting things off. Artist, writer, inventor and architect Leonardo Da Vinci is a known genius who has the world's most famous painting on display in the Louvre Museum in Paris. His creative production spans a wide range of projects: illustrations, sketches and human anatomy exploration were all part of his arsenal. He never focused on one thing at any given time. During Da Vinci's lifetime, there are less than twenty surviving paintings attributed to him and several of them are unfinished. Two of his most important works, the *Battle of Anghiari* and the *La Scapigliata*, were not completed and only survived as copies. *The Virgin of Rocks* took him thirteen years to complete and the infamous *Mona Lisa* as many as sixteen years. Da Vinci gained a reputation for being unreliable. He consistently started projects only to abandon them, leaving a trail of incomplete paintings and sculptures behind. Da Vinci leaves behind a lingering question for us: why do we procrastinate?

The common assumption is that procrastination is an act of laziness or incompetence. The truth lies in our biology, where there's a constant back and forth in our brain between the limbic system and the prefrontal cortex. The limbic system is the oldest and more dominant part of the brain, automatic in its response.

It's the part of the brain that tells us it's too hot to be outside or the air conditioning is too cold. It also tells us to run from unpleasant tasks; a function which performs our basic survival instincts.

The prefrontal cortex, on the other hand, is the part of our brain used in our conscious decision-making. It is the weaker part of the brain, where decisions require laboured thought. Quite often, the limbic system wins, putting us in a position to procrastinate. We need to use the prefrontal cortex to consciously engage in tasks. The challenge we face is retraining the brain so the limbic system reacts differently to tasks we undertake.

When we procrastinate, it's often because our future self wants something different than our current self. The inconsistencies of future and current time help us understand why we buy a gym membership and don't go, or why we always go to bed late and wake up tired the next morning. For example:

Future Self: Wants to have a clean kitchen without any dishes
Current Self: Feels like watching TV on the couch
Future Self: Wants to lose weight
Current Self: Feels the need to eat unhealthy foods
Future Self: Wants to change careers
Current Self: Finds it too difficult to create an avenue

The time required to achieve something and the time we expect to achieve it is inconsistent. When we set goals for ourselves, we act as our future self, envisioning what we seek based on long-term rewards. Our current self seeks instant gratification without the long-term payoff.

To stop procrastinating on something, we need to move the long-term rewards and consequences into the present.

Imagine You're working on a project for your manager and have a deadline to meet. It slowly starts to creep up and you start to feel the anxiety and guilt build as you continue to postpone the task each day. The night before it's due, you start working on it and submit it before the due date. The pain of procrastination reaches a tipping point, where you finally begin to work on it the night before. Once you took action, the guilt and anxiety let up and started to decrease. When procrastinating, the course to action is always an uphill battle. But once you take action, the path then becomes a ride downhill. The challenge is to reduce the gap between intention and action. When we look for motivation, we are waiting for something to happen. The key is to take action in order to attract motivation as opposed to waiting to find that feeling to act. There are different strategies we can use to overcome our relationship with procrastination.

Strategy #1: Seek immediate rewards. Bring your future rewards into the present moment. We can bundle good long-term behaviour with behaviour that feels good in the short term. For example, if you want to spend more time with friends and family, include the person in a specific activity you enjoy. If it's going out for dinner, choose a restaurant you enjoy and invite that person. Perhaps you want to eat healthy. You can watch your favourite TV show while preparing healthy foods. Or maybe your goal is to spend less money, so every time you buy clothes or over indulge in items, you price match the amount you spend into your savings account. Knowing how much you consume causes you to spend less and save more.

Strategy #2: Find a commitment trigger. A commitment trigger helps lock us into a specific action in the benefit of changing our behaviour to reach a goal. If you want to get healthy, you might remove all the junk food in your house. If you want to stop mindlessly using your phone, you might delete apps that restrict your productivity. There are two basic features for a commitment trigger to become effective. First, those who commit must voluntarily elect to use them. A commitment trigger requires us to be self-aware enough in the gap between our current goals and our likely future behaviours. Second, the commitment trigger must associate the consequences with our failure to achieve a goal. We need to ensure we apply this strategy in a healthy, beneficial way.

Strategy #3: Pomodoro technique. This strategy helps us become more effective in our actions. It works by setting a twenty-five-minute timer while acting on one task. Complete as much as you can within that time. After the twenty-five minutes is up, you then have a five-minute break. After four cycles, have a fifteen- to thirty-minute break. This technique is effective whether you're an office worker, a student writing a paper or just spring cleaning your house.

Irrespective of the strategy we use, we need to remind ourselves that motivation will always come second to action. We often get confused between the need for an incentive to act and having a system for us to proceed with less thought. Our motivation is there to carry us through effortlessly and build momentum. Instead of trying to overcome procrastination through sheer willpower, we should focus on strategies so we can retrain our brain to reduce the gap between intention and action.

CHOOSING YOUR PRIORITIES

Are you a time optimist or a time realist? No matter if you're unemployed, a part-time worker, a stay-at-home parent, an entrepreneur or a student, we all have twenty-four hours in our day. Many of us aren't realistic in what we can accomplish each day. We cram as much as we can into our schedule thinking we can do it all. But the reality is, we can't keep this up and have enough time for what levels us out, like exercise, friends, family and a decent sleep. Your schedule doesn't have to be like that. You can prioritise what's important and find you'll get those things done more often.

• • •

We can make our priorities action based. Ask yourself, what makes my life successful? Think of your answer in terms of what you value. Success may look like having enough time to play a sport while working long hours or the ability to see friends and family often. Now reshape this question to, am I allowing enough time to be successful? Use your answer by making a list of priorities that can be action based. Here are some examples:

Priority#1: Spend time with family and friends
Action #1: Leave the office earlier, dedicate one night a week to catch-up

Priority#2: Exercise more
Action #2: Hire a personal trainer or go to the gym with a friend

Priority#3: Read more
Action #4: Have a book located on your bedside table so you're reminded every night

Of course, priorities can change. Sometimes a life event occurs, you might get ill or a new relationship arises. There will be times where you may require your time management to be devoted to your health or times you may have to reduce your work output to let your relationship grow. Living out what's important to you requires constant balancing and reassessing. As long as you're basing your actions and priorities on the first question—what makes my life successful?—you'll always have the ability to focus on the time spent prioritising what you love.

Self-Sabotaging Emotions. You've been able to draw up priorities and actions to implement, but defining them is only half the solution. Sticking to them is the true test. Perhaps you've started going to the gym but found yourself slacking a month later. Or maybe you've been chasing a dream of finishing a degree only to drop out after a semester. Learning to invest your time wisely is not just about coming up with an action plan, it's also identifying the underlying emotions that affect how you behave in an area you have prioritised. If those emotions aren't addressed, self-sabotage can occur.

One of the most common emotions when starting something new is fear. We have all experienced it—being scared to look foolish or thinking we will fail. The problem with fear is that it causes us to lose focus on what's important. Achievement is always on the other side of fear. Take time to acknowledge what you feel and identify what it is that scares you. Once you do that, fear can lose its power and motivate you to take action. Strong emotions can disrupt the actions you take on your priorities. By addressing and acknowledging how you feel, emotions can become your best allies.

Set Realistic Expectations. We regularly misjudge the amount of time it takes to accomplish a task. There's been plenty of times where I'll assume it will take me an hour to research ideas. I often use this assumption because it's what I'm consistently aiming for, but it doesn't happen every time. I get distracted or I'll stop and think about whether or not my what I'm reading is of value. It can lead me to think I'm not doing enough when, in reality, I'm doing plenty.

A time optimist takes on too much commitment, thinking they can accomplish it all in their allocated time frame. The problem with being overly optimistic with time is that it can consistently leave you stressed and overwhelmed when reality sets in. So what do you do? You need to set realistic expectations. As easy as it is to say, setting realistic expectations is much more challenging to do. There are a couple of effective tools you can use to set goals of how you manage your time.

Strategy #1: Find your peak performance time. I referenced earlier the importance of identifying when you best perform. To reiterate that point, break down your day into typical time slots. Over the course of the week, rank each slot in order from your most productive to least productive. This is an effective time management strategy to help your days become less demanding and to gauge your energy levels.

Strategy #2: Evaluate how realistically your time is being assessed. After finishing a task, evaluate how long you thought it would take versus how long it took. If completing a similar task in the future, use the data from the previous task to create a new time expectation.

Strategy #3: Use a "future time" approach. Is what you're doing right now helping you or hurting you in the future? How do the projects you take on today help tomorrow?

Of course, some expectations come from outside influence, like your boss giving you an extra twenty hours of work and expecting it done in one week. You arrange a meeting and advise you're unable to get everything done in time, so you'll prioritise the most urgent tasks. It's okay to say no to your boss to be realistic. A lot of the time we say yes to something and find a way to get it done. But the downside of that approach is that it creates more unwanted stress for ourselves.

Improve Your Simple Routines. Simple routines are a sign of effective time management. They're the blueprint of each individual to achieve peak performance. Routines reduce stress because there are less decisions you're required to make in a day. Routines can be looked at in a couple of ways. They can be used for the workaholic to reduce their hours or they can be for the individual to become more productive. How can you implement a routine?

Step One: Work out what you want to do. The list of priorities and actions you made earlier? Focus on that.

Step Two: Visualise your routine and any possible barriers. If you want to exercise after work, look into what could possibly stop you from doing that.

Step Three: Put it into practice. The routine may feel unnatural at first, and you may want to let the mental blocks get in the way. Keep going, and don't think it has to be perfect. It will often be messy, but consistency creates results.

Most of us live impulsively, where decisions throughout the day become automatic. Time is a commodity, so we need to spend it wisely. Make action-based priorities, set realistic expectations and create a simple routine. Your time management will be more effective, stress will reduce and you can live a more effective life.

33

ORGANISED SUCCESS

Ivy Lee, a businessman and public relations pioneer, consulted for some of the world's largest industrial firms. Most notably known for consulting the Rockefeller family, Lee would transform companies, increasing their efficiency and performance. The Ivy Lee Method began in 1918, when the owner of Bethlehem Steel Corporation, Charles Schwab, sought out Lee to boost productivity in the organisation.[1]

"How can I get more things done efficiently?" Schwab said.

Lee responded, "Give me fifteen minutes with your top executives".

"What's the cost?" Schwab asked.

"Nothing at all," Lee responded.

"If it works, send me a cheque for whatever you feel the improvement was worth. If you didn't improve, send me nothing".

Three months later, Schwab noticed a significant improvement in productivity by using a simple method Ivy Lee told the executives. "At the end of the night, write down your most important tasks to do the following day, listing them in order of importance. When the next day arrives, work on those tasks in order of value". Schwab gave Lee a cheque for $25,000 (the equivalent of $425,000 today).

When Lee spoke with the top executives at Bethlehem Steel, it took him fifteen minutes to explain the system Schwab found so life-changing. The system went like this:

1. After your workday, write down the six most important tasks you're required to do the following day.
2. Number the list in order of true importance.
3. When you arrive at work the next day, work only on the first task. Only once it's finished, move on to the second task.
4. Approach the rest of the list this same way, and repeat the process each day.

It's a simple strategy, which is what makes it so effective. We often believe the most straightforward methods are too good to be true. We look for new and improved ways to achieve results even when a basic system can provide us with direction and consistent performance. We can boost productivity in our career and personal life from the simple strategies.

From the moment you wake up, you're making a decision. Whether it's to lay in bed, sleep in some more or get up and have a shower, your brain is now active. The Ivy Lee Method helps you understand how you will attack the next day. By understanding what's required the evening before, you have already translated to your brain how you will perform when you wake up the following day. Being consistent in writing down your six priorities helps reduce decision fatigue because you're not constantly thinking about what to do next. The outcome results in a productivity boost and an increase in mental energy.

A lot of us see multitasking as a way to improve productivity. We can find ourselves getting more things done, but we may not be getting the right things done. Multitasking is productivity masking, meaning we use other tasks to view ourselves as busy and hardworking, but in reality, we're not reaching our potential in any given area. The Ivy Lee method promotes single-tasking, whereby focusing on one thing creates a direction to optimal performance in that task. The more we practise single-tasking, the more influential the results.

A Starting Point

Starting a task can be extremely difficult when you don't know where to start. Not knowing where to begin offers a reason to procrastinate and tricks you further into not starting. The Ivy Lee checklist provides a new direction and an improved way to focus your energy. By starting on one task, it makes it easier to not only complete that task but to complete the others effectively as well.

The Ivy Lee Method has become a valuable strategy that has helped me reduce stress while building an author business. There was a never ending to do list: weekly emails, social media marketing, communicating, writing, implementing new ideas, etc. I would focus on the most important task that day and work my way down. It's a sensible and practical solution to close the gap between overwhelm and progress.

Challenges Moving Forward

The message and method are simple. Do the most important things each day. Of course, we know there will be distractions, emergencies and uncontrollable factors that come our way. But the act of doing what's essential each day when there are no distractions make it easier to bounce back once you come across the uncontrollable factors that require your attention.

If you would like to be more efficient, make life easier for yourself. If you're a writer, download software that helps you become organised and effective. If you work in an office and succumb to constant email checking, remove email notifications. By making it easier on yourself, your list of six important items becomes exceedingly doable and brings about effective results.

The rule is simple: simple organisation, maximum success.

34

OPTIMAL PERFORMANCE: SUMMARY

- Effort, trust and consistency will *always* exceed talent. It's not about achieving everything right away. It's about organising longevity in your actions.
- Having something to reach provides direction because our actions determine our reality. Focusing too much on life-changing goals tricks your mind into taking on more than you can handle. Focus on the small progression points to achieve greater rewards.
- To find peak performance, set an intention before each activity and start to identify your moments of focus throughout the day.
- Energy is the battery for all our thoughts and behaviours. Become aware of how you currently distribute it and work towards balancing out different energy dimensions.

PILLAR VI

LIVING IN THIS WORLD

"Life is a storm that will test you unceasingly. Don't wait for calm waters that may not arrive. Derive purpose from resilience. Learn to sail the raging sea". – Unknown

As we reach the final pillar of the book, each section has previously opened with a story—stories of incredible individuals and collectives representing the overarching theme of each pillar. Pillar Six: Living In This World begins a little differently. This story is dedicated to my significant other Nicole and her remarkable resilience, to her late mother Shelley, and to her father Neil. It's a reminder that there will be times when we're confronted with uncontrollable events, bad luck and the pressure of navigating uncharted waters.

Shelley spent most of her life living in Northam, a small country town in Western Australia. Over the years, Shelley had overcame several health issues. She was always determined to fight through the challenging scenarios she was presented with. The most significant journey came in 2016 when Shelley underwent a kidney transplant. When the doctor found a kidney, they tried to call Shelley to give her the news. She was watching a live football game with her husband Neil and didn't answer the phone. Nicole's contact details were listed as the emergency number, so the doctors managed to reach her with the good news. The doctor informed Nicole that a kidney was available for Shelley, but she couldn't get a hold of either of them. The hospital needed to confirm as soon as possible. Nicole got straight on the phone, calling both parents' mobiles repeatedly. Adrenaline started to build.

Nicole called Amanda, her sister in Queensland. They both kept calling but still no answer. Nicole decided to call the football stadium, but that only led to being put through to the food stands and time was of the essence. There were at least seventy phone calls that went completely unanswered. A friend suggested to Nicole that she message the stadium on Facebook. Nicole sent a random request to the stadium staff to go to the box Shelley and Neil were in, ask for Shelley and let her know that a kidney was ready and she needed to answer her phone. Shortly after, Nicole's mum responded to the missed calls, and they were on their way to the hospital. The Facebook message had gotten through.

Nicole met Neil and Shelley at the hospital, adrenaline at a high from finally receiving the good news—they had long waited for a new kidney.

Shelley underwent kidney transplant surgery a few hours after leaving the football game. Following the successful transplant on 16 July 2016, Shelley stayed with Nicole for post-op care and monitoring. They started a routine together of pancake breakfast and morning conversations.

The kidney transplant gave Shelley a new lease on life. It gave her freedom as she could travel with Neil on holidays and attend work conferences while creating new experiences with family and friends. Although there was more freedom in the years that followed, Shelley was met with more challenges. Nicole and I visited the family house in Northam for Christmas in 2021. It was the first Christmas spent in Neil and Shelley's new house that they had only moved into a few weeks prior. Unfortunately, Shelley battled with circulation issues and couldn't get the blood flowing in her leg. She was in significant pain and confined to the couch. The pain got worse; through early 2022, Shelley was in and out of the hospital. After each trip home from the hospital, there would be a brief respite before experiencing more pain in her leg. Before too long, Shelley was back in the hospital. Her vascular and kidney doctors tried to relieve pain and provide circulation through different procedures. After they failed, Shelley was told there was a high chance her leg would have to be amputated. It was news that had to be processed. After some discussions with Shelley's doctors, they would try her toes instead of removing the leg. This would at least allow Shelley to build strength in her legs and still be able to walk.

After a couple more amputation surgeries, despite being met with extremely challenging circumstances, Shelley still maintained her kind-hearted spirit. She joked around with nurses, told them stories about her travels, spoke about her family and was always interested in their lives.

But just when everyone thought she could build her strength back, she started to decline again—still in significant pain. The doctors had to closely monitor her situation as she began rapidly losing strength.

Then came the call no one wanted to hear. Shelley didn't have long left to live. Her kidneys were failing at speed, and what could have been done had already been done.

For Nicole, Neil and the family, we again had to process the news as we would prepare for our last moments with Shelley and living life beyond what we're used to experiencing.

Shelley sadly passed away in palliative care on the eve of 2 June 2022 from kidney failure.

She was an incredible, kind and loving person who gave her heart to everyone she loved. Shelley lived a simple but rewarding life. She cherished working with Neil at the liquor store every day, always enjoyed going to the local pub for a feed, and loved being in the company of family and friends. A remarkable woman in her own right.

There's a reality we must face as we get older and gain more experience: we will experience uncertainty, struggle to find the right balance and wonder at times whether or not the juice is worth the squeeze.

Living In This World is the final pillar of living a rewarding life. The following chapters provide awareness of the common challenges and experiences faced each day we wake up. We get so caught up in progress and performance that we forget what it's like to exist and respond to the world we're presented with. As you move through these final chapters, consider Shelley's story as a reminder to never take the simple things for granted. The time spent with family and loved ones, the dinners and drinks with friends, keeping in touch with your inner child and the moments you spend on your own can provide you with unexplainable energy and joy. And that is one of the ultimate trademarks of living a rewarding life. Because without it, we forget who we are. But with it, we remain centred, spirited and thriving.

35

PRACTISE PATIENCE

When did you last find yourself frustrated? The WiFi dropping out, waiting in an extremely long line, being stuck in traffic and plane delays are all common scenarios that lead us to a feeling of impatience and annoyance. Even when we attempt to slow down and allow for tolerance, those changes are temporary, and we revert to our old way of living in a fast-paced world.

We feel impatient because humans have ingrained the thought that we can perform faster with each new invention. And with each new invention, we receive one new dent in our frustrations. Impatience arrives when a scenario doesn't align with our habits. There are some things you want to achieve: lose weight, create a business, build a house, buy a car, etc. But where we fail comes from previous habits of convenience. When we don't see results immediately, we stop performing the actions that get us from A to B. And when we optimise our life for convenience, we set ourselves up for consistent frustration.

To become more patient, examine your current thoughts about waiting for results. Do you think about anything other than your ultimate goals? What else do you enjoy that would complement patience and persistence? The time we spend with our thoughts, wondering why success isn't on its way, can be substituted with other small enjoyments life brings. That might be a hobby, spending more time with friends and family or embracing downtime earned by your previous hard work. When you immerse yourself in one particular goal with specific success, everything else around you becomes less important. While tunnel vision can help you hone in and focus on a particular task, it has the potential to block other opportunities and possibilities which improve your life. Start learning and focusing on the behaviours and actions which complement your ultimate goal. With this expanded focus, you begin to enjoy the process and journey itself because you don't mind the direction you're heading in.

When working towards something big, we make certain changes to help get us there. Those changes could be as small as waking up an hour earlier or as big as moving cities to start a new career. When noticing recent life changes, we adapt and direct our habits to what becomes familiar. The upside to this is we're going with, not against, the changes we make. The downside, though, is that these adapted habits bring an increased sense of impatience. Our propensity to perform new actions in the face of change means we open ourselves up to frustration when we don't immediately see the results we want. Improve patience by directing your focus towards focus and practise—the two unquestionable equations that equal progress.

In the late 1970s, Dr Salvatore Maddi, a University of Chicago researcher, studied employees who worked at Illinois Bell, a company owned by AT&T, to understand how employees thrived through stress and to isolate those characteristics to help others who didn't.[1] The study lasted several years and followed four hundred and thirty male and female supervisors, managers, executives and frontline staff. In 1981, deregulations and a change in company structure hit. Illinois Bell went from twenty-six thousand staff to half of that in one year. Dr. Maddi's test was still allowed to progress through these changes and lasted until 1987.

Upon completing the study, results showed that two-thirds of the employees showed compelling health deficits and performance in the face of workplace stress. There were records of heart attacks, strokes, poor performance reviews, depression, divorces, substance abuse and considerable anxiety. The remaining third who maintained health, happiness and performance thrived on the instability surrounding them. Those thriving employees saw the restructuring and changes at the company as new opportunities. They also chose to view all changes as a platform for learning, whether good or bad. They remained engaged instead of being personally attacked when forced to pivot. They performed positive actions in their work, recognising opportunities to fix long-standing internal problems that wouldn't have otherwise been dealt with. But the employees who struggled were found to have spent their time and energy frustrated and impatient. They consumed themselves with how things used to be.

In our lives, there will always be new changes, and we will feel nostalgic and prefer situations return to how they were, which is part of human life. But what is also a prerequisite for working through challenging times is accepting instability but still moving with purpose.

Have a committed attitude to learning. Be okay with trying to influence outcomes even though you will experience struggle, and view challenges as new opportunities rather than roadblocks that lead to powerlessness.

When we focus on learning something new or building toward something big, impatience becomes one of our biggest enemies. When trying to live a rewarding life, we sometimes want to progress quicker than we are. But practise being patient. When we make ourselves wait, we build resilience. Building patience helps create wealth in our lives. Become patient in the gym, become patient in the workplace and become patient in relationships. Patience is to be happy with our work and not fight process and progression. When we do this consistently, our energy and focus become much more valuable and results begin to flow.

36

PURSUE A CAREER INSTEAD OF A JOB

How you think about the work you do makes a difference. A career incorporates both a personal and professional life, allowing you to enjoy each day. But a job is limited in its ability to bring fulfillment because it's considered something we have to show up for—the enjoyment comes from leaving the job when the day's over. Because earning money is a prerequisite for living, how we view the money we make doesn't always align with our direction. Ask yourself, am I working a job or am I taking advantage of my career?

Often, we get asked, what do you want to do in life? Or, what do you want from your professional career? Most of us are unsure. There's nothing wrong with not knowing. But we second guess ourselves. We question our destination. When we see others get a promotion or friends having children and getting married, we look at our own lives, even if just for a split second. It's human nature. In moments of uncertainty and self-doubt, we can amplify our own life and think about the professional direction we're headed. If you find yourself in a position where you don't enjoy your job, don't *leave* before you leave. In other words, don't mentally check out before sending in the resignation letter. Find your career direction as if you would through a compass—work from checkpoint to checkpoint. There are four steps to explore which helps keep you motivated and on track towards a career worth having.

Step One: Set Your Destination. What are your interests? Do they align in the industry you're in? Think about what you want most from your career and ask, what is one thing I can do that will help me get moving in the right direction? Is it getting a promotion or starting a small business? You might still enjoy your current role but would like more energy and freedom. The likelihood of taking action increases when you have a destination. Identify where it is you want to go. Find one small, time-based action to get you moving and be open to learning anything and everything to get you there.

Step Two: Analyse Your Current Position. What do you currently offer in your career? What skills do you have that benefit others? Do you appreciate those skills? Identify your strengths and question whether they're being utilised. Your potential is defined by your ability to learn, apply and translate skills into goals and aspirations. Aligning attention with intention breeds progress. If you feel something is blocking you from reaching your potential, analyse the situation so you can plan your route.

Step Three: Plan Your Route. What do you have to do to get to your destination? Are you required to begin learning from the bottom? If it's the case, work on managing your ego as you start progressing. Or do you already possess skills which you're looking to take to the next level? Then work to become an expert and help as many people as you can. To effectively plan your route, identify how you can reach your destination by understanding what's required of you. You might have to take on unpleasant roles, but like how a rookie becomes a professional, focus on small improvements over time and you will find a way.

Step Four: Recognise the Hurdles. There will be plenty of challenges on the way, but avoid self-sabotaging, burning bridges and burnout. There will be predictable obstacles too, so find out what they will be. Relocating? Extra qualifications? Dealing with difficult people? How we reach our destination depends on how well we handle the hurdles.

WHEN TO LOOK FOR A NEW CAREER

Suppose you consistently show up to your job tired and unmotivated. How are you spending your evenings and mornings? When you aren't enjoying your job, it can be amplified by an inconsistent routine. Do you get enough sleep? Continually run late? Feel less productive? Getting out of old patterns opens you up to new ideas and new incentives. Take time to review your bad habits and replace them with something new and improved. Additionally, motivation is always a struggle when you're on the verge of burnout. The reason we're overworked and overwhelmed in our career comes down to a few things:

1. You're good at your job and prefer to control all tasks
2. Company culture promotes burnout and overwhelm
3. Your ineffective with your time

If you have improved other areas of your life and find you're not enjoying what you do more than before, you should consider moving on. Working on your professional direction helps pinpoint different aspects of your career. It opens up the opportunity to either stay the course and be successful or make the switch and be better for it.

37

BECOME SOMEONE WHO CREATES

Our ability to create stems from our capacity to generate conscious thoughts into existence. The words you write, the reels you make, the home you design, the holiday you plan—these are all examples of generating thoughts to better serve us.

I remember when I was traveling home from a trip away with friends. My friend, Matt, asked me if I was creative. "Nope, not at all" was my response. I had always perceived creativity as a natural ability. What I didn't understand was that creativity is something you can learn and acquire at any age. I've always enjoyed writing, learning and reading. Once I changed the way I thought about creativity, my ideas and mind started to open and flow. The remarkable thing about creativity is its ability to take you places you never thought you'd go. The significant improvements we make allow us to continue generating new thoughts, ideas and confidence so we're able to put them out into the world that resonates with our direction in life.

As we navigate through this world, it's easy to assume creative thoughts are simply big ideas that are out of reach. In reality, those big ideas you dream about have been willed into existence from your small thoughts. Your subconscious mind has been developing over time to create ideas that push you in the direction you want to go. One of the biggest barriers to acting on our new ideas stems from how we think of ourselves and our ability to create. This is why creativity should be recognised as a skill and something we can learn. Every person who has produced significant work has long before produced significant thoughts. There are a few ways we can practise creativity: opening our minds, surrounding ourselves with inspiration and encouraging bad ideas.

Open Your Mind. By opening your mind, you can powerfully unleash creativity and tap into ideas beyond your imagination. By cultivating a mind that is open to new thoughts and ideas, there is no ceiling to your creativeness. A closed-minded person lives life on autopilot; they reject and block out new ideas if those ideas are not in line with their beliefs. People with open minds want to experience more of the world and are more receptive to what life has to offer. Practise listening to others views and opinions to open up awareness and opportunity for ideas.

Surround Yourself with Inspiration. Soak up all the inspiration you can find. Read a great book, walk in nature and learn from people that inspire you. If we are never exposed to what fascinates us, it limits our mind to be open and more creative. I find my inspiration from different sources. I'm a sociable person, and I'm lucky to have friends who have great wisdom and positivity. I don't rely on my friends as a sole inspiration source. I delve into books, my thoughts and reputable professionals in their field. But each source promotes newfound ideas.

Encourage Bad Ideas. Without bad ideas, we don't know what the good ones are, so it's important to throw all our ideas into the ring and get feedback so you can refine what works and what doesn't. It's better to have fifty bad ideas and one good one instead of no ideas at all. Sometimes one bad idea primes our mind to think of a good idea. Alternatively, the idea we perceive to be bad is, in fact, a remarkable thought.

Creativity is an amazing skill. It allows us to put ourselves in a positive zone, giving us a sense of purpose to build and work towards something. We all have creativity within us. Take time to immerse yourself into newfound ideas and you can reach potential you never thought possible.

38

FIND YOUR BALANCE

We're always on the quest to find the perfect work-life balance to free up our time to do the things we love. Children, family, friends, health and activities are key areas we direct our attention to. The downside is that we only have twenty-four hours in one day. The average human spends eight to ten hours a day working, not to mention commuting to and from work. Include six to eight hours of sleep, and that leaves us with very little time and energy to focus on everything else. American comedian and author David Sedaris came up with The Four Burner Theory.[1] It's a different take on how we can find the right balance in life. Imagine an old stove top in your house. You have a four-burner stove, and each burner represents an area of your life.

Burner 1: Represents your family
Burner 2: Represents your friends
Burner 3: Represents your career
Burner 4: Represents your health

The Four Burner Theory states that to be successful, you're required to cut off one burner. To be really successful, you're required to cut two. When you think about it:

- A business owner can focus solely on their career, working overtime while neglecting their health.
- A friend can focus on their mental well-being so health becomes a priority, and career aspirations are on the back burner.
- A young adult can travel overseas, focusing on creating new friendships. Health and friends then become the focus and career opportunities get sacrificed.
- A couple can have a child together, so the family burner gets turned up. When they begin to focus on being parents, the friends burner is turned down.

Can you run on all four burners simultaneously and achieve what you seek? One thing to remember is that life has trade-offs. You'll be required to sacrifice something to benefit another area at each life stage. Finding what combination of dedicated time we spend in each stage requires acknowledging what you value. You can then prioritise your burners in line with living a balanced life. We all live differently and all share different values. Habits expert James Clear came up with three options to help find the right balance for whichever stage of life you're in:[2]

Option One: Who Can You Delegate To?
We outsource minor parts of our lives all the time:

- We take public transport to work because it's quicker than sitting in traffic.
- We buy ready-made meals from the shop to save time cooking.
- We hire a personal trainer so we can become motivated.
- We employ a virtual assistant to save time and improve other areas of our business/life.

- We find a babysitter so we can spend quality time with friends or use the time to focus on our health.

The advantage of outsourcing is that you can keep the burner running without spending much time on it. Just be sure the burner you choose is meaningful and doesn't jeopardise the future performance in the area you're outsourcing.

What areas can you delegate to free up your time for more essential things?

Option Two: Embrace Your Limitations

Many of our lives are spent wishing we had more time to do XYZ—I wish I had more time to get to the gym, or I wish I had enough time to make dinner. A way to manage this problem is to shift your mindset to a new location. Instead of wishing there was more time, maximise the time you have. How much time are you limited to, and how can you be as effective as possible in that limited time?

- I only have time to exercise two hours a week. How can I get in the best shape possible?
- I only have one hour to spend with my partner each night. How can I make it meaningful?
- I only have time to write for thirty minutes every other day. How can I use this time to publish a book?

The change in mindset focuses on getting optimal results out of what's available to you instead of worrying about the time you don't have available. Well-designed limitations help improve your performance and productivity. The disadvantage of embracing your limitations means you're operating your burners at an average rate. If you're looking to build a business, it may take you twice the amount of time. If you're looking to improve a skill and practise that skill less frequently, you will improve at the rate you practise.

You must find what matters to you and consider whether you're willing to delay the rewards for a balanced life.

Option Three: Work In Seasons

Instead of focusing consistently on a work-life balance, divide your burners into seasons that focus on a particular area. Imagine a boxer who spends twelve weeks in a training camp preparing for a fight. They train two to three times a day in the gym, get adequate sleep and eat a strict diet. The rigorous training puts them in supreme condition to make the fighting weight limit. Once the fight is over, they relax and focus on other areas of their life. They start to make time for their friends and family, they don't train as much and they become more relaxed in their diet.

The burners are working in seasons. Seasons change throughout your life. In your early twenties, it might be easier to make more time for exercise and partying every weekend. The friends and health burners are peaking. But when you get to your thirties, you might have children, so the health burner and friends burner get turned down, and the family burner gets more gas.

Ten years pass, and you may decide to take action on a business idea you've thought about, so the burners change again. It all comes down to what you're willing to give up in order to get back.

One thing to acknowledge is that life rarely allows us to keep all four burners running at once. You don't have to give up on what you seek because there will be a time in life when it works for you. Is that time now?

The benefit of understanding The Four-Burner Theory is being able to use these options to make more informed decisions on how we choose to live. We can't have it all (right away). Every choice has a cost. Are the choices you make worth the cost?

39

UNIVERSAL LESSONS TO LIVE A GOOD LIFE

There are always aspirations to live a full life. Whether it's increasing your income, starting a family or travelling the world, we want to live well. I've learned that it doesn't say anything about you and your capabilities if you're not feeling too great about your direction. It simply comes down to your perception and way of thinking. As we come towards the end of the book, remind yourself that the way you perceive what you do determines your actions. And those actions summarise your reality.

Although we all walk different paths, there are universal lessons that help us stay the course of living a rewarding life

Lesson #1: Stick to a Routine That Works

Throughout the book, I've advocated for having positive routines in your life. It's proven that routines control stress, make more time to relax and increase overall health. A solid routine provides structure and builds on forward-moving habits, creating momentum to live a better life. Routines will carry you through the days when you don't have the strength to carry yourself. When creating a routine, the key is to develop consistent and regular daily patterns that move you in the direction you want to go.

Within our routines, life will always get in the way. The point is to hold onto our most productive times for our most energy-driven tasks and our least effective times with mundane tasks. Allow for specific events. Whether it's a social gathering, doctor's appointment or a work dinner, having a daily routine gives you the energy to show up and keep your days flowing smoothly, despite any hiccups. And remember: keep updating and refining your routines as you continue to improve.

Lesson #2: Be Grateful For What You Have

When you stop and think about what you already have, your perception of what's not going well changes for the better. Take time out of the day to focus your time and attention on what you appreciate. It can be the simplist things, like cherishing your friends who are there supporting you. Sometimes it's easy to feel bad because you're going through a rough time and things aren't going your way. However, no matter how bad your situation is, there's always something to be grateful for. Just like the old Persian proverb said, "This too shall pass".

Lesson #3: Look Forward to Getting Older

People call me crazy, but I genuinely look forward each year to getting one year older. Ageing will always be part of life. Be proud of improving experiences and advancing your knowledge. Here's a list of reasons why you should look forward to getting older:

- You stop caring about what others think
- You'll have great memories to share
- You'll start building lifelong friends
- You become wiser
- You understand yourself more

Lesson #4: Rest Often

Managing your energy is one of the biggest keys to performance and output. You might find students constantly tired or corporate office workers burnt out. Society tells us to be busier for longer. Performance is set up through overtime hours and a curriculum where students learn all day and work on assessments and homework all night. Of course, some people pull this off, but burnout eventually catches up. You can't use your energy 100% of the time. If we try, we make poor decisions and risk losing clarity. Take small breaks throughout the day and longer holidays throughout the year. Productivity will increase, and the overwhelming stress will decrease.

40

LIVE A REWARDING LIFE

If you've made it this far, I want to thank you. It means you've found this book interesting enough to act on benefiting from your time in this world. Not everyone makes it to the end of a book, and I'm honoured you've stuck with me for this long.

We all aspire to live a good life. You and I have an almost unlimited number of opportunities in this world. Living a rewarding life is about ultimately finding what's important to you, setting your destination and taking enjoyable action so you can walk the pathway of progression, success and all-time happiness. And the beauty of it? Your path is as unique the next person's path. They may share the same characteristics and similar goals, but your journey cannot be replicated.

Trust in the pillars covered throughout this book, and I guarantee that you will live a rewarding life, as defined by you.

Choose to do something remarkable. Do it for yourself. Do it for those important to you, but most importantly, do it because it's possible.

READ.THINK.LISTEN

Each week I send out a free newsletter called Read. Think. Listen. It's aimed to enhance the trajectory of your life and improve how you show up each day. There's three parts of what you will receive each Friday:

1. Tips on human performance and how you can perform at your best.
2. Two sets of wise words dedicated to the art of living.
3. Two inspirational quotes from others.

Join me and many others as we continue to live a rewarding life. You can join at: www.blakedevos.com/read-think-listen

This is also a more direct way to stay up to date with my upcoming books.

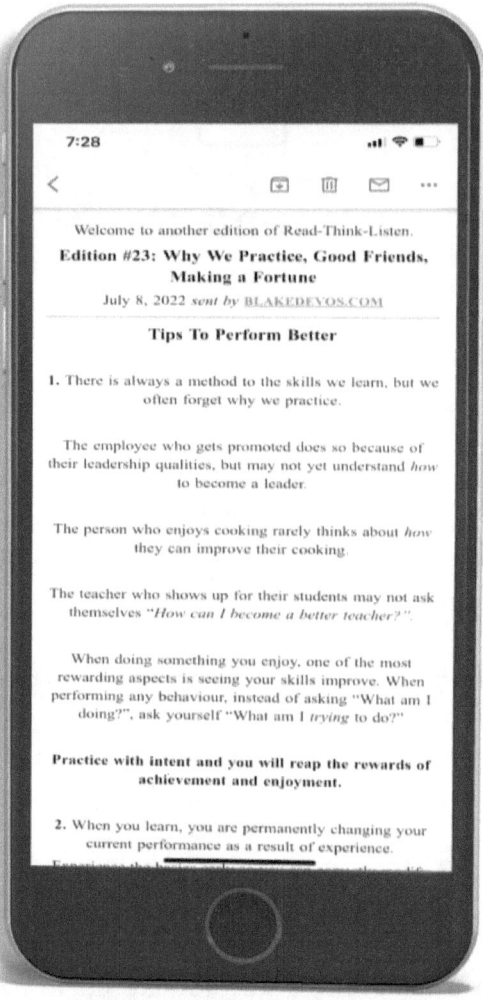

blakedevos.com/read-think-listen

ACKNOWLEDGMENTS

Firstly, this book would not be possible without the works of others that I've heavily relied upon. Thank you to those authors, speakers, researchers and professors who have given me and many others a platform to communicate knowledge and ideas in our own voice. I have done my best to credit your influential work. Secondly, at the beginning of the book I wrote a dedication to who this book was for. I'd like to acknowledge those people one more time. Thank you to my parents Christine and Henk. You have always supported me in anything I pursue.

Thank you to my wonderful partner in life, Nicole. We do life so well together and I'm eternally grateful to be the one that gets to share it with you. You've been with me through the ups and downs of life and I'm glad you're always there to put things into perspective when doubt starts to creep in.

Thank you to my best mate Anthony. We've shared many beers together as I've sat and dribbled thoughts, and often pointless ideas that have come to fruition and succeeded. You were there when I first started writing all those years ago, and you're still here after publishing my first book.

Thank you also to Matty D and Laura G. You both read the first draft opening to this book and gave some honest and sound advice. Matt, I appreciate your support and creative advice you've given me over many years. And LG, you've given me confidence in my writing. From when we first sat down together, you gave an honest assessment in my structure and flow that led to how I approach the entire process of writing. I'm deeply grateful and I'm glad to call you both friends.

And speaking of friends—Thank you to all those who supported this book. I'm lucky to have such incredible people in my life. Good friends are hard to come by. But when you have people who support your passions up close and from afar, you continue to progress and improve. I'm forever grateful to have friendships forged with you all.

Thank you also to Nanna Carroll for being a wonderful grandparent. You have always been a true support for the whole family and deserve nothing but love and joy.

And to Grandad Callaghan, my pal. Whenever we visit you, I'm reminded that the simple things are the most important. You're the happiest person I know with the happiest of hearts and am still trying to figure out how you know so much about football.

Thank you to my cover designer, Mary Ann. You were unbelievably patient in getting the artwork right and bringing my vision to life on the front, back and spine.

Thank you to my launch team for getting this book off the ground. You've been a great help and provided incredible feedback.

Thank you to my editor, Carmen. You brought this book to life and met every single deadline I asked for. I'm blown away by your detail and brilliance in not only the work you do, but the kindness you show and constructive feedback you provide.

And lastly, thank you to you—the reader. Without you, this wouldn't exist. Without you, I wouldn't write this book. Without you, this wouldn't mean anything. I truly hope you go out there and become a creator. Forge your own path and live the rewarding life you ever deserve.

Until next time—Reward yourself. Go and create a life you're proud of.

PLEASE LEAVE A REVIEW

Thank you ever so much for reading this book. I hope it added some value to your life. Even if one sentence made an impact, I've done my job as a writer. Reviews are important for the wider reader community in the books they choose to engage. If you could please take a moment and leave an honest review on your favourite store, it would mean the world.

Thank you.

RESOURCES

2. Appreciate Your Emotions

1. **Driving related deaths.** Deonandan R, Backwell A. Driving deaths and injuries post-9/11. *Int J Gen Med.* 2011;4:803-807. doi:10.2147/IJGM.S27049
2. **September 11 attacks.** Myers DG. Do we fear the right things? APS Obs. 2001;14:3. [Google Scholar]
3. **Negative facial expressions.** Ekman, P. (2005). Facial Expressions. In Handbook of Cognition and Emotion (eds T. Dalgleish and M.J. Power). doi:10.1002/0470013494.ch16
4. **Emotional responses.** LeDoux J. Rethinking the emotional brain. Neuron. 2012 Feb 23;73(4):653-76. doi: 10.1016/j.neuron.2012.02.004. Erratum in: Neuron. 2012 Mar 8;73(5):1052. PMID: 22365542; PMCID: PMC3625946.

3. Change And New Experiences

1. **Unusual preparation.** 'Harry Garside explains his unusual boxing preparation'. August 27, 2022. https://www.sen.com.au/news/2021/08/10/bronze-medallist-harry-garside-opens-up-on-extraordinary-olympic-preparation/.

5. The Antidote To Fear

1. **Greatest fear.** JK Rowling. Text of JK Rowling's Speech. June 5, 2008. https://news.harvard.edu/gazette/story/2008/06/text-of-j-k-rowling-speech/
2. **Fear and snakes.** Uri Nili, Hagar Goldberg, Abraham Weizman, Yadin Dudai, Fear Thou Not: Activity of Frontal and Temporal Circuits in Moments of Real-Life Courage, Neuron, Volume 66, Issue 6, 2010, Pages 949-962, ISSN 0896-6273, https://doi.org/10.1016/j.neuron.2010.06.009.

6. Start To Live

1. **Stop Worrying, Start Living.** Dale Carnegie's discussions with Earl P. Haney. "Classic Stories On Conquering Worry". http://www.conquerworry.org/uploads/2/4/5/5/24554406/classic_stories.pdf.

8. Decision Mechanics And The Process Of Deciding

1. **Judges decision making.** Imhoff, R. and Nickolaus, C. (2021), Combined Anchoring: Prosecution and defense claims as sequential anchors in the courtroom. Leg Crim Psychol, 26: 215-227. https://doi.org/10.1111/lcrp.12192
2. **Historical petrol prices.** Australia's average petrol prices in 2003 from the Australian Institute of Petroleum. https://fleetautonews.com.au/historical-pump-prices-in-australia/
3. **Measles vaccine.** Rao TS, Andrade C. The MMR vaccine and autism: Sensation, refutation, retraction, and fraud. Indian J Psychiatry. 2011 Apr;53(2):95-6. doi: 10.4103/0019-5545.82529. PMID: 21772639; PMCID: PMC3136032.
4. **Survivorship bias.** The Royal Institution. Abraham Wald and the missing bullet holes. https://www.rigb.org/explore-science/explore/blog/how-not-be-wrong. An independent charity dedicated to connecting people through science.

9. Having Too Many Choices

1. **Decision fatigue.** Pignatiello GA, Martin RJ, Hickman RL Jr. Decision fatigue: A conceptual analysis. J Health Psychol. 2020 Jan;25(1):123-135. doi: 10.1177/1359105318763510. Epub 2018 Mar 23. PMID: 29569950; PMCID: PMC6119549.
2. **Impact of decision fatigue.** Vohs, Kathleen & Baumeister, Roy & Twenge, Jean. (2005). Decision Fatigue Exhausts Self-Regulatory Resources — But So Does Accommodating to Unchosen Alternatives.

10. Be The Architect

1. **Fukushima disaster.** Government and public response to risk communication. Murakami M, Tsubokura M. Evaluating Risk Communication After the Fukushima Disaster Based on Nudge Theory. Asia Pacific Journal of Public Health. 2017;29(2_suppl):193S-200S. doi:10.1177/1010539517691338
2. **Risk communication on individuals.** Blood cell count. Sakuragi, S., Moriguchi, J., Ohashi, F. *et al.* Reference value and annual trend of white blood cell counts among adult Japanese population. *Environ Health Prev Med* **18**, 143–150 (2013). https://doi.org/10.1007/s12199-012-0304-8
3. **Food downsizing.** Schwartz J, Riis J, Elbel B, Ariely D. Inviting consumers to downsize fast-food portions significantly reduces calorie consumption. Health Aff (Millwood). 2012 Feb;31(2):399-407. doi: 10.1377/hlthaff.2011.0224. PMID: 22323171.

11. When Overthinking Occurs

1. **Choking under pressure.** Ellis, L., & Ward, P. (2022). The effect of a high-pressure protocol on penalty shooting performance, psychological, and psychophysiological response in professional football: A mixed methods study. *Journal of sports sciences*, 40(1), 3–15. https://doi.org/10.1080/02640414.2021.1957344
2. **Perfectionism and quality of work.** Harari, D., Swider, B. W., Steed, L. B., & Breidenthal, A. P. (2018). Is perfect good? A meta-analysis of perfectionism in the workplace. *Journal of Applied Psychology*, 103(10), 1121–1144. https://doi.org/10.1037/apl0000324

12. Learn To Play The Long Game

1. **Marshmallow test.** Mischel, Walter and Ebbe B. Ebbesen. "Attention in delay of gratification." Journal of Personality and Social Psychology 16 (1970): 329-337.

13. Decide To Make An Impact

1. **Making an impact.** Ryan White 1988 panel interview article. March 9, 1988. https://www.edweek.org/education/panel-hears-aids-victims-story/1988/03
2. **Ryan White CARE Act.** Institute of Medicine (US) Committee on the Ryan White CARE Act: Data for Resource Allocation, Planning, and Evaluation. Measuring What Matters: Allocation, Planning, and Quality Assessment for the Ryan White CARE Act. Washington (DC): National Academies Press (US); 2004. 2, Overview of the HIV/AIDS Epidemic and the Ryan White CARE Act. Available from: https://www.ncbi.nlm.nih.gov/books/NBK216136/

17. Setting Effective Goals

1. **Mcconaissance.** Matthew McConaughey: What happened to the 'McConaissance'?. 23 November, 2019. https://www.nzherald.co.nz/entertainment/matthew-mcconaughey-what-happened-to-the-mcconaissance/MBLG7SKJNKBFONVAOLRSBNXG2Y/
2. **Exercise routines.** Milne, S., Orbell, S., & Sheeran, P. (2002). Combining motivational and volitional interventions to promote exercise participation: protection motivation theory and implementation intentions. *British journal of health psychology*, 7(Pt 2), 163–184. https://doi.org/10.1348/135910702169420

18. Powerful Stages Of A Personal Challenge

1. **Outside world.** Jiang, L., Stocco, A., Losey, D.M. et al. BrainNet: A Multi-Person Brain-to-Brain Interface for Direct Collaboration Between Brains. *Sci Rep* **9**, 6115 (2019). https://doi.org/10.1038/s41598-019-41895-7

IV. Developing Effective Habits

1. **Behan World Championships.** Keiran Behan of Ireland To Compete In 3 Gymnastic Events. 26 July, 2012 https://www.nytimes.com/2012/07/27/sports/olympics/against-odds-kieran-behan-of-ireland-to-compete-in-3-gymnastics-events.html

23. The Relationship With Your Environment

1. **Forces which drive our behaviour.** Lewin, K. (1938). *The conceptual representation and the measurement of psychological forces.* Duke University Press. https://doi.org/10.1037/13613-000
2. **Visual environment.** Fisher, A. V., Godwin, K. E., & Seltman, H. (2014). Visual Environment, Attention Allocation, and Learning in Young Children: When Too Much of a Good Thing May Be Bad. Psychological Science, 25(7), 1362–1370. https://doi.org/10.1177/0956797614533801

24. Starting Small

1. **Uber's strategy.** How to Make Positive Changes that Stick with Wendy Wood. The Psychology Podcast. YouTube. May 22, 2020. https://www.youtube.com/watch?v=KXX5lZS2Akk

25. Your Rewards And Motivators

1. **Receiving rewards.** Ashleigh Barty interview 24 March, 2022. https://www.theguardian.com/sport/the-nightwatchman/2022/mar/24/ash-barty-tennis-cricket-golf-nightwatchman-grand-slams

V. Optimal Performance

1. **Value of Leicester.** Transfer market statistics. Squad value 2014. https://www.transfermarkt.com/premier-league/marktwerteverein/wettbewerb/GB1/plus/?stichtag=2014-12-15

27. Initial Belief

1. **Struggle to sustain exercise effort.** The Biggest Loser. The failure of dieting. http://www.nytimes.com/2016/05/08/opinion/sunday/why-you-cant-lose-weight-on-a-diet.html

28. How To Practise

1. **The Polgár sisters.** Robert W. Howard,Does high-level intellectual performance depend on practice alone? Debunking the Polgar sisters case, Cognitive Development, Volume 26, Issue 3. 2011. Pages 196-202, ISSN 0885-2014, https://doi.org/10.1016/j.cogdev.2011.04.001.(https://www.sciencedirect.com/science/article/pii/S0885201411000335)
2. **IQ and Performance.** Bloom, B. S. (1985). Generalizations about talent development. In B. S. Bloom (Ed.), *Developing talent in young people*. Ballantine Books.
3. **Deliberate practice.** Ericsson, Karl & Krampe, Ralf & Tesch-Roemer, Clemens. (1993). The Role of Deliberate Practice in the Acquisition of Expert Performance. Psychological Review. 100. 363-406. 10.1037//0033-295X.100.3.363.
4. **World record typist.** Rose Fritz. The Wonderful World Of Typewriters. From Robert Messenger 24 July, 2013 https://oztypewriter.blogspot.com/2013/07/rose-louisa-fritz-world-champion-typist.html

29. The 1%

1. **Toyota and Kaizen.** The Toyota Way- Our Process. https://www.toyotafleetmanagement.com.au/about/our-process. A statement on Toyota's continuous improvement initiatives.

30. Energy And Performance

1. **Manage your energy.** Harvard Business Review. Manage Your Energy, Not Your Time. October 2007. https://hbr.org/2007/10/manage-your-energy-not-your-time

31. Productive Living

1. **Childrens behaviour.** Booren LM, Downer JT, Vitiello VE. Observations of Children's Interactions with Teachers, Peers, and Tasks across Preschool Classroom Activity Settings. Early Educ Dev. 2012 Jul;23(4):517-538. doi: 10.1080/10409289.2010.548767. PMID: 25717282; PMCID: PMC4337404.
2. Mills A. (2019). Helping students to self-care and enhance their health-promotion skills. *British journal of nursing (Mark Allen Publishing)*, 28(13),

33. Organised Success

1. **Ivy Lee.** The Unseen Power: Public Relations, a History. https://catalogue.nla.gov.au/Record/205021. This was sensationally adapted by James Clear in his article https://jamesclear.com/ivy-lee. A common productivity practice in the business world.

35. Practise Patience

1. **Stressed employees.** Maddi, S. (2016) Hardiness Is Negatively Related to Gambling. *Open Access Library Journal*, **3**, 1-4. doi: 10.4236/oalib.1102250.

38. Find Your Balance

1. **Four burner theory.** David Sedaris. Laugh, Kookaburra. August 17, 2009. https://www.newyorker.com/magazine/2009/08/24/laugh-kookaburra.
2. **Burner options.** The Downside of Work-Life Balance. https://jamesclear.com/four-burners-theory. A formidable approach to work life balance. Piggybacking off David Sedaris, James Clear has brought a practical approach which I duly credit to find our work-life balance.

ABOUT THE AUTHOR

Blake de Vos is an author in the non-fiction self help genre. His primary writing interest is in human performance and bases himself online at www.blakedevos.com. Blake lives in sunny Perth, Western Australia with his partner Nicole and dog Oliver. He enjoys sport, reading, writing, boxing, pubs and travelling.

www.ingramcontent.com/pod-product-compliance
Lightning Source LLC
Chambersburg PA
CBHW020857020526
44107CB00076B/1883